International Conflict and Collective Security

WILLARD N. HOGAN

International Conflict and Collective Security

The Principle of Concern in International Organization

UNIVERSITY OF KENTUCKY PRESS

Copyright 1955

To My Parents

THE CONTROL of man's violence against man presents to modern society its problem of problems. In the atomic age a capacity to deal with the most devastating type of conflict—international war—is crucial to human welfare and even to the survival of civilization. Nations have become interdependent in technology and economy, but world political organization is based on a system of sovereign states now divided into hostile camps armed with absolute weapons. What principle of organization offers the best hope for the settlement of international disputes and the control of international violence? Should reliance be placed on power diplomacy, collective security, supranational government, or some other approach to a stable international order?

This book presents the results of a case study of the "principle of concern," underlying a system of collective security, as it has developed since the first World War. In making such a case study it is necessary to consider two separate but interrelated questions. First, to what extent has a principle of political organization been formally and constitutionally accepted? Second, to what extent has it been relied on in practice and made actually effective? In other words, it is my purpose to analyze relevant trends in international organization from the viewpoint of both structure and function.

I owe to many persons and books a greater intellectual debt than can be acknowledged in bibliography and footnotes. To Professors Amry Vandenbosch, University of Kentucky, and Quincy Wright, University of Chicago, I wish to express my gratitude for their helpful advice over a period of years. Any errors of fact or fallacies of interpretation are, of course, my own fault and responsibility.

WILLARD N. HOGAN

Contents

CHAPTER ONE

The Principle of Concern

MODERN attempts to deal with the problem of war by means of collective security represent a reliance upon the "principle of concern" in international relations. This principle may be defined as a recognition that conflict among the members of a group affects the entire group and that a unilateral resort to violence against any member constitutes an offense against all members. It involves the idea of organization to preserve peace, an idea which lies at the basis of every political community.

During the century prior to World War I the nations sought to preserve peace by the balance-of-power policy, the Concert of Europe, and general co-operation. The concept of the balance of power was that no state should become strong enough to dominate the others, this goal to be achieved by defensive combinations against any nation threatening to upset the equilibrium. Each country could preserve its independence and maintain its security by co-operating with others for the same purposes. In unity the weak might find strength to oppose the strong. However, the policy of balance and counterbalance degenerated into a system of opposing alliances, finally dividing Europe into two armed camps.

The Concert of Europe undertook to maintain a kind of unity under the supervision of the Great Powers, on the basis of the *status quo* established at the Congress of Vienna, and in general to regulate the affairs of the continent to prevent a disruption of the peace. The concert worked through a series of

conferences after the Napoleonic Wars, and the idea was re-
vived later in connection with such conferences as the Con-
gresses of Paris in 1856 and of Berlin in 1878.

The Hague conferences of 1899 and 1907 represented another attempt to implement an interest in the preservation of
peace. On the whole their purpose was to deal with the problem of war in two ways: the provision of alternative procedures for settling disputes and limitations to prevent needless
suffering of noncombatants, prisoners, the wounded, and others.
The agreement that a tender of "good offices" was not to be
considered an unfriendly act implied that nations might have
a concern in the settling of disputes not involving their own
immediate interests.

In the nineteenth century and up to World War I the relation of nations at peace to those at war was dominated by the
principle of "traditional neutrality." Upon an outbreak of hostilities third states had the choice of participating as belligerents or of assuming a status of neutrality. In general the requirements of the law of neutrality were understood and accepted. The prevailing idea was that neutral countries had
certain rights against the belligerents and certain duties toward
them. Failure to fulfil the obligations of neutrality brought the
risk of reprisals from any belligerent adversely affected. It is
true that there were controversies over particular rules and
recurrent violations; nevertheless the principle of traditional
neutrality found an increasingly secure place in the system of
international law and organization.

According to the nineteenth century conception resort to
war was a fact outside the realm of law, like an earthquake.
International law recognized no right of passing judgment on
the legitimacy of participation in war by states. A collective
interest in the maintenance of peace might be expressed, but
no penalty was attached to recourse to war. No matter what
the circumstances of an outbreak of war, nations that did not
elect to participate were to observe neutrality, the basic principle of which was impartiality between belligerents. It is important to recognize, however, that to some extent this view

reflected an interest in the maintenance of peace. Historically the principle of traditional neutrality originated in a demand for the right to stay out of war, and it tended to limit the geographic scope of warfare. It did not attempt to prevent or to extinguish the conflagration, but it did try to keep the blaze from spreading.

The Covenant of the League of Nations represented the first formal incorporation of the principle of concern into international organization. This was a stage in a long development rather than a completely novel idea, but the extent of the change revolutionized the prevailing attitude toward international conflict. The emphasis shifted from mild restraint to determined prohibition, from the national interest to the common concern. International solidarity was asserted. The sovereign right of unilateral warmaking was qualified. The idea of protection by co-operation was generalized from a system of shifting *ad hoc* alliances to collective security. Instead of some against others, it was to be all against any who broke the peace.

Formal agreement on a general principle means little unless its implications are made effective in practice. It is important, therefore, to give careful attention to the application of the principle of concern in the development of international organization and in the policies of nations. Analysis of the record, as set forth in the following chapters, reveals a general acceptance in the drafting of the League Covenant, an immediate movement toward restriction and limitation, a period of modified application beginning in 1925, a disintegration during the 1930's, and a reaffirmation with the establishment of the United Nations.

CHAPTER TWO

Acceptance: The League of Nations

ACCEPTANCE of the principle of concern by the League of Nations after World War I was a crucial event. The succeeding course of international organization has been marked by controversies over the principle, its soundness and its meanings; by the successes and failures of action based upon it; by its development and interpretation; and even by the alternatives suggested for it.

Organized peace as a war aim had been expressed in Great Britain as early as 1914, when Prime Minister Asquith spoke of "a real European partnership based on the recognition of equal right and established and enforced by a common will."[1] Professed war aims of this type found a sympathetic response in the United States—increasingly so as the sentiment of neutrality gave way to participation on the side of the Allies. Theodore Roosevelt had already suggested, in accepting the Nobel Peace Prize in 1910, that "it would be a master stroke if those great powers honestly bent on peace would form a league of peace, not only to keep the peace among themselves, but to prevent by force if necessary, its being broken by others."[2] This "league for peace" idea had received wide acceptance by the early months of the war. In April, 1915, a "Central Organization for a Durable Peace" was created at The Hague. On May 3, 1915, the British "League of Nations Society" adopted a program calling for "a treaty binding members to peaceful settlement of all disputes" and for united action to see that "every member shall abide by the terms of the treaty."

The plan of the American "League to Enforce Peace," stated by former President Taft at Cleveland, Ohio, on May 12, 1915, had four major points: a court for justiciable disputes; a conciliation commission for other disputes; conferences for the development of international law; and an agreement "that if any member of the League shall bring war against any other member of the League, without having first submitted the question, if found justiciable, to the arbitral court provided in the fundamental compact, or without having submitted the question, if found non-justiciable, to the Commission of Conciliation for its examination, consideration and recommendation, then the remaining members of the League agree to join in the forcible defense of the member thus prematurely attacked."[3]

On May 27 a year later, President Wilson, speaking before the League to Enforce Peace, endorsed the idea of a universal association of nations to keep the peace and asserted the willingness of the United States to become a partner in such an enterprise. Apparently Wilson at the time hoped that such a league might be created on the basis of "peace without victory." This approach was followed by the Lansing note of December 18 to the belligerents, asking for a statement of peace terms. An appeal for "peace without victory" was reiterated by Wilson himself as late as his address to the Senate on January 22, 1917. Shortly afterward this particular war aim was discarded, but the idea of a concert of powers after the war was retained, to be accomplished by the consent and partnership of the nations after removing the impediment of the "Hohenzollern tryanny." In his war message to Congress in April, Wilson stated that the object was to "vindicate the principles of peace and justice

---

[1] *Speeches by the Earl of Oxford and Asquith, K.C.* (New York, 1927), 218.

[2] Quoted by Felix Morley, *The Society of Nations*, 5-6.

[3] For accounts of "peace as a war aim" see Morley, 3-29; William E. Rappard, *The Quest for Peace since the World War*, 18-59; Margaret E. Burton, *The Assembly of the League of Nations*, 1-28.

in the life of the world as against selfish and autocratic power and to set up amongst the really free and self-governed peoples of the world such a concert of purpose and of action as will henceforth ensure the observance of those principles."[4]

The idea of a concert of powers, of the concern of all in any resort to war, was not only accepted by the United States and Great Britain, but in one form or another it found its way into the professed aims of all major belligerents. The degree of enthusiasm varied, of course, and sometimes support of the idea was a perfunctory gesture, with a propaganda appeal and perhaps some support from individual statesmen or segments of public opinion. All in all, the interest was "keener in the United States than in Great Britain, keener in Great Britain than in France, and keener in France than in any other of the European Great Powers."[5]

The war aim of an organized and enforcible peace was included in the armistice terms by the last of the famous Fourteen Points: "A general association of nations must be formed under specific covenants for the purpose of affording mutual guarantees of political independence and territorial integrity to great and small States alike."

At the Peace Conference the objective of a general association for mutual guarantees was translated into the Covenant of the League of Nations. At this stage the principle of concern was asserted. Article 11 of the Covenant stated in its first sentence, "Any war or threat of war, whether immediately affecting any of the members of the League or not, is hereby declared a matter of concern to the whole League, and the League shall take any action that may be deemed wise and effectual to safeguard the peace of nations."

This provision of Article 11 may be regarded as the heart of the League Covenant; it was a basic concept underlying the territorial and political guarantees of Article 10, the settlement procedures of Articles 12 to 15, and the enforcement clauses of Article 16. The existence of the League of Nations, with

---

[4] *President Wilson's State Papers and Addresses* (New York, 1918), 378.
[5] Rappard, 42.

the system of collective security which it embodied and sym-
bolized, depended upon an assertion that any war is of common concern to all nations. For the first time the principle of
concern was accepted and formally incorporated into international law and organization.

Article 11 was strengthened at succeeding stages in the development of the Covenant, gradually coming to occupy a
more central place in the entire scheme.[6] The concept seemed
to evolve as first, an interest in peace; second, a belief that
peace, to be maintained, must be enforced; and finally, an
affirmation of the principle of concern as the basis for the enforcement of peace. In preliminary outlines of the Covenant
a provision bearing a close resemblance to the eventual language of Article 11 appeared first in Colonel House's draft of
July 16, 1918, which stated, "Any war or threat of war is a
matter of concern to the League of Nations and to all the
Powers, members thereof." Wilson's first draft provided, "Any
war or threat of war, whether immediately affecting any of the
Contracting Powers or not, is hereby declared a matter of
concern to the League of Nations and to all the Powers signatory hereto, and those Powers hereby reserve the right to
take any action that may be deemed wise and effectual to
safeguard the peace of nations."[7]

The draft completed by the Commission on the League of
Nations on February 14, 1919, stated the principle of concern
substantially as it was finally accepted in the Covenant, but
differed in providing that in the event of war or threat of war
"the High Contracting Parties reserve the right to take any
action that might be deemed wise and effectual to safeguard
the peace of nations." The Cecil-Wilson agreement of March
18, 1919, resulted in changing the words "reserve the right to
take" to the much stronger term "shall take."[8] Article 11 became, therefore, a clear and definite expression of the solidarity

[6] On the constitutional development of the League, including the various
preliminary plans, Morley's *The Society of Nations* is invaluable; the relevant
documents are presented in David Hunter Miller, *The Drafting of the Covenant.*
[7] Miller, II, 7, 14.   [8] Morley, 131-32.

of the members of the League, with the maintenance of peace made formally obligatory upon them rather than permissive and discretionary.

Article 11 of the Covenant was the formal recognition of the social fact of world interdependence, that the peace of the world is of concern to the whole world simply because a war anywhere has repercussions everywhere. Peace was a paramount concern for nations which feared that they might be victims of aggression, for neutrals who under modern conditions of warfare might be affected almost as much as the belligerents, and for third states because of the tendency of war to spread.[9] The prevention of war had come to be recognized as one of the foremost duties of government. The presumption of change only by peaceful means was adopted, and it was hoped that resort to aggression could be met by overwhelming resistance by members of the League acting as a group.

In two important respects the League of Nations' plan for peace departed from centuries of precedents. First, it represented a formal and governmental acceptance of an international scheme for the prevention of war. Earlier peace plans, by contrast, had been put forth by individuals or small groups of people. The nearest approach to the League idea was probably the Concert of Europe after the Napoleonic Wars. But this was carried out by a series of conferences based on the agreement of statesmen, with no formal delimitation of scope or constitutional provision for continuance. Such peace measures as were incorporated into international law and organization were not designed to prevent, but rather to restrict, warfare.

Geographic and temporal limitations had been placed on war in the Middle Ages by such devices as the Truce of God and the Peace of God. The principle of traditional neutrality,

[9] "Since the Thirty Years' War there have been fourteen periods in which war existed with a great power on each side for over two years. There were only three of these major war periods . . . in which a single one of the great powers remained at peace throughout the period." Quincy Wright, A Study of War, 240.

which reached its highest development during the nineteenth century, was essentially, so far as its aspect of peace maintenance was concerned, a device for the geographic limitation of war. The nineteenth and early twentieth centuries also saw the development of restrictions designed to reduce the frequency of warfare and to ameliorate the suffering. Alternative procedures for the adjustment of international controversies were supplied in the form of good offices, conciliation, inquiry, mediation, arbitration, judicial settlement, and "cooling-off periods." If war unhappily came despite these devices, there were the conventions for the protection of noncombatants, prisoners, and the wounded. The flag of truce and the Red Cross were to be respected. These methods of pacific settlement and of ameliorating human suffering might be called procedural limitations on warfare. Resort to war was viewed as an extralegal fact, as a permissible method for use in international controversies, but some concern about its recurrence and effects was shown in the principle of traditional neutrality and in the various restraints on the initiation and conduct of hostilities. The time-honored geographic limitation on fighting was retained, but instead of being based primarily on the sanctity of churches and monasteries, it took the form of certain protections for nations not involved in a war. The temporal limitation, that fighting might not take place on certain days of the week, was largely abandoned. More reliance was put in procedural limitations. At the best, however, there was no challenge to a state's right to wage war if it decided that its interest so required. Such limitations on unrestricted warfare as existed could be enforced only through persuasion, good faith, or reprisal.

A second difference between Article 11 and early peace plans which had found any formal or governmental acceptance was the interest in conflict as conflict. There is a real, though often wavering and nebulous, distinction between aggression viewed as a threat to one's own direct interest and as a threat to the peace and stability of the group. Third states have often objected to a resort to war because of what a belligerent might gain, because of the possible consequences for the balance of power and other considerations. The principle of concern requires third states to object to any resort to war simply because it is a resort to war—thereby extending interest in consequences from the immediate effect upon national rights to the effect upon the stability and order of the international community. The assumptions are that the best security is a secure environment and that the best protection against aggression is membership in a society which prohibits aggression. It is a question of whether a nation shall prepare to defend itself or co-operate in an attempt to remove the necessity for defending itself.

Probably the effective scope of Article 11 was limited by the provisions of Articles 12 to 15. It is also true that there were "gaps" in the Covenant, so that some wars remained licit. Nevertheless, Article 11 in itself was an unqualified acceptance of the principle of concern, and this article expressed the basic attitude of war prevention through international solidarity which lay at the heart of the League and the entire system of collective security. Limits on the scope of Article 11 arose in prescriptions of the manner and relative completeness of its application. They did not prejudice the fact that Article 11 enunciated the principle to be applied. A number of disputes actually were brought before the League by invoking this article in preference to those which marked out the procedural steps to be taken.[10] In any event, permissible war could exist only within the gaps of the Covenant. Some degree of regulation over international conflict was obtained by virtue of defining the conditions under which war would be prohibited and those under which it might be permissible. In principle, the gaps in the Covenant would be analogous to a national legal system which might continue to permit the duel and other

[10] Eighteen disputes were submitted to the Council under Article 11 by 1929. See T. P. Conwell-Evans, *The League Council in Action*, 10-121, 278-81. The Sino-Japanese dispute first came before the League when China invoked Article 11 on September 21, 1931. Ethiopia appealed to the League under Article 11 in January, 1935. For an account of international disputes handled by the Assembly, see Burton, 284-374. By the end of 1939 the League had dealt with 66 political disputes, in 30 of which Article 11 was invoked alone or in connection with other articles. Wright, 1429-31.

forms of forcible self-help. Of course, such an analogy would be valid only if the League had become effective within the scope of its authority, and then only subject to the great difference in degree between gaps in international as compared with national control of conflict.

At any rate, even the gaps involved a regulation and definition of their boundaries, and in turn an implication existed that the gaps might be narrowed by a reinterpretation of the boundaries. All things considered, it is clear that there was general acceptance of the principle of concern at the end of World War I, with the precise extent of its incorporation and application left open for future development. The legal and organizational basis for control of international conflict was adopted. The question then became: To what extent would formal acceptance be matched by functional effectiveness?

CHAPTER THREE

Limitation

No SOONER had the principle of concern been accepted than its limitation began to develop. This retreat from general acceptance took place in several ways. First, there was a geographic limitation when membership in the League of Nations did not become universal. The original hope and intention was that the League would function on a world-wide basis. Obviously, however, this could not take place unless all important nations undertook to carry out the obligations of the Covenant. Second, there was a limitation by interpretations incompatible with the implications of full acceptance. This weakened the basic assumptions on which the League was built and later provided a rationalization for dilatory and ineffective action. Third, there were certain survivals of the principle of traditional neutrality. These clearly limited the principle of concern, since by definition a declaration of neutrality is inconsistent with attempts to apply adverse differential treatment against a nation which resorts to war. Finally, the negotiations concerning proposals for disarmament, security, and arbitration rejected the principle of concern as a feasible basis for practical action.

It is important to trace these developments in some detail, in order to examine the extent to which the principle of concern became functionally effective. In following this analysis, the precise relationship between various key terms must be kept in mind. The *principle of concern* refers to an attitude toward conflict among the members of a group; it is the fundamental concept on which the others are based. *Collective security* may be defined as "general co-operative action for the maintenance and enforcement of peace."[1] *Differential treatment* means that third states will assist a victim of aggression and penalize the aggressor, in contrast to an impartial position as required under the principle of traditional neutrality. The *League of Nations* was the organization, or institutional means, by which the principle of concern was to be implemented and the necessary action taken. The question of functional effectiveness of the principle of concern, therefore, has been one of developing a system of collective security and strengthening the League of Nations (and later the United Nations).

1. NONMEMBERS OF THE LEAGUE

Refusal of the United States to become a member of the League can well be taken as the point of departure for considering the trend toward limitation and restriction of the principle of concern. Chronologically this is the first step, as the crucial vote in the United States Senate came on March 19, 1920,[2] only a little more than two months after the League of Nations officially came into existence and almost eight months before the first meeting of the Assembly. Moreover, this action on the part of the United States withdrew the support of the leading proponent just as the organization was coming into existence. The United States under the leadership of President Wilson had taken the initiative in the acceptance of the principle of concern in international organization. It also took the initiative, with the repudiation of Wilson's leadership, in the limitation of that principle.

The absence of the United States from the League left a huge gap in that geographic inclusiveness which would be

[1] See Chapter VI, section 3.
[2] For an account of the issue in the United States and the action of the Senate, see Denna F. Fleming, *The United States and the League of Nations, 1918-1920*, and his *The United States and the World Organization, 1920-1933*, 3-41.

one of the essential prerequisites to a complete acceptance. But the effect was more than one of a lack of geographic inclusiveness. The implications for the two leading members of the League at the time—France and Great Britain—were great.

At the Peace Conference France had been primarily interested in arrangements for its own future security. Opposing its ideas for the basis of postwar international organization was the United States. The latter proposed a system of collective security to achieve a warless world; France was more vitally interested in a firm guarantee against the menace of a militant and aggressive neighbor.[3] One advocated a general, the other a specific, approach. And the general system was accepted by France with the understanding that the specific guarantees were included as a part of the arrangement.

The Covenant of the League, based on the Anglo-American draft, was developed at the Paris Peace Conference in 1919 by the Commission on the League of Nations.[4] At the eighth meeting of this commission, on February 11, 1919, the French representative brought up the issue of an international force to compel respect for the Covenant. "The argument that the League must establish its members in a position of *sécurité nationale*, with the implication that otherwise each State must be the sole judge of its armaments requirements, was strongly stressed by the French delegates at this meeting. From that day to this the French position has not deviated from the thesis that if the League does not absolutely insure the security of its members, those members are not justified in trusting the efficacy of the Covenant as a way of permanent peace."[5]

At this same meeting of the commission the French proposed three amendments to the draft of the Covenant: (a) to require as a condition of admission to membership in the League effective guarantees of an intention to respect the Covenant

[3] This difference can be accounted for by considerations of geography and national interests. See Rappard, *The Quest for Peace*, 100-102.

[4] For a succinct account of the work of this commission, see Morley, *The Society of Nations*, 77 ff. The relevant documents are given in Miller, *The Drafting of the Covenant*.

[5] Morley, 108.

and to emphasize the obligation of a new member to conform
to the League's regulations on armaments; (b) to establish an
international control of troops and armaments; and (c) to apply sanctions to enforce a unanimous opinion of the Council
on a dispute submitted to it. The French delegation again
proposed amendments dealing with an international armed
force during the meeting of a drafting committee on the next
day (February 12). One day later another debate on the
French amendments took place in the Commission on the
League of Nations. On this occasion the French representative
said, "One of the conditions necessary for the League of Nations to be able to impose peace, is that the whole world knows
that it has the means to impose it and to impose it at once."[6]
The same French contention was continued and elaborated at
the twelfth meeting of the commission on March 24.[7]

The final meeting of the Commission on the League of Nations was held on April 11, 1919. Apropos of the formal
approval of Article 15, paragraph 7,[8] the French representative
commented, "The whole idea of obligation has now disappeared. It will, therefore, be necessary to continue and to
conclude separate alliances, inasmuch as the League admits its
inability to offer a formal guarantee of protection to its own
members."[9] Again, when the Covenant was formally adopted
by the Peace Conference, the French delegate spoke for the
rejected amendments, urging a system for the mutual verifica-
tion of armaments and the establishment of a permanent military commission in connection with the Council's responsibility
for maintaining peace. In accepting the Covenant without
these amendments, France expressed the hope that they might
be embodied in the Covenant at a later date.[10]

Even a cursory examination of the French attitude toward

  6 Miller, I, 256.   7 Morley, 155-60.
  8 "If the Council fails to reach a report which is unanimously agreed to by
the members thereof, other than the representatives of one or more of the
parties to the dispute, the members of the League *reserve to themselves the
right to take such action as they shall consider necessary* for the maintenance
of right and justice" (italics added).
  9 Morley, 195.   10 Same, 207.

the League of Nations reveals a development from indifference or even unfriendliness to acceptance and support only as the principle of a collective guarantee was accepted in return and as there appeared to be a willingness on the part of Great Britain and the United States to back up such a guarantee. The major efforts of the French in the drafting of the Covenant were devoted to strengthening the guarantees which would operate to protect the French frontier in case of attack. They sought a machinery of sanctions to make their security more reliable. The cleavage between the French and the Anglo-American positions and concepts were bridged over by compromises and by concessions to the French point of view. Rejection of the Covenant by the United States destroyed that bridge. The assurances actually obtained by France were those of support from Great Britain and the United States through the League and of mutual support in case of aggression. American nonparticipation rendered valueless those assurances for which France had been persuaded to relinquish her more drastic demands as against Germany. The French basis for accepting the League, that it should have force to protect the security of France, was largely eliminated by the action of the United States in rejecting the Covenant.

The attitude of the British government was more in harmony with American concepts of the nature of the League than was the case with France, especially since there had been a great deal of Anglo-American co-operation in preparing the early drafts of the Covenant. The effect of American absence from membership was therefore different for Great Britain than for France. To Great Britain fell a heavy share of the responsibility for underwriting collective security. Without the co-operation of the United States the British government could not fulfill this obligation. What if the American government should insist on its neutral rights in opposition to a British fleet engaged in blockade operations against a state designated as an aggressor by the Council of the League?

Sir Edward Grey had said in 1916 that unless the United States was a member of a league of nations, and a member that could be depended on to intervene, the peace of the world would be no more secure in the future than it was in 1914.[11] Stanley Baldwin said in 1934 that he would not permit the British navy to be used for an armed blockade of any country until he knew in advance what the position of the United States government would be. Between the times of these two statements the British continually showed reluctance to go "all out" in undertaking obligations of collective security because possible nonco-operation or opposition by the United States would impair the efficacy of sanctions, disrupting the trade of participating nations to no gain in security.

Abstention of the United States from the League of Nations weakened the security of the nation most conscious of the need for security and exposed to greater risks in guaranteeing security the nation which would have the heaviest responsibility in that task. It made the danger greater and the means for meeting the danger less potent. How, then, should one appraise the real significance of American action on the League system of collective security and therefore on the acceptance and the limitation of the principle of concern? President Wilson had said in January, 1920, "The maintenance of the peace of the world and the effective execution of the treaty depend upon the whole-hearted participation of the United States."[12] There can be no question that failure to receive that participation was a heavy blow. But there is no reason to believe that this one blow was necessarily fatal or that the single fact of rejection by the United States conclusively doomed the League to failure from the very beginning. No doubt the chances for success were lessened, but it does not follow that the chances were destroyed.

There is no way to analyze and evaluate the real effect of American rejection on the League except by inference. There can be no record of the League with American membership to compare with the record without it. Yet even though the

[11] See John Fischer Williams, *Some Aspects of the Covenant of the League of Nations*, 31.
[12] *Messages and Papers*, II, 1162.

question is not susceptible of definitive proof, it does offer possibilities of a rather convincing conclusion. Let us look at a few typical opinions on this question. The neutral Swiss student, sympathetic observer, teacher, and for some time participant in the affairs of the League, William E. Rappard, considered the blow a stiff one indeed, as if a symphonic concert should be offered with the composer-conductor suddenly prevented from appearing.[13] Two other statements may be quoted from the same authority:

"One may either contribute to the enforcement of the blockade or render it ineffective and therefore impossible. Political isolation and nonco-operation, whatever their motives, are in fact obstruction."[14]

"The members of the League are inhibited from granting each other the necessary measure of mutual protection because the lack of universality of the League leads them to fear external complications if they should faithfully carry out the pledges of the Covenant."[15]

The proposed amendments to the Covenant demonstrated that American absence influenced League policy by encouraging efforts to modify the Covenant to please the United States and by making member states unwilling to undertake obligations which might bring them into conflict with the United States if put into practical effect.[16]

Sumner Welles from the vantage point of the problems of another peace said: "Another major reason for the failure of the last peace was the refusal of the United States to enter the League of Nations and to ratify the Treaty of Versailles, and the beginning of a period of withdrawal by the American people from any share of responsibility in international affairs."[17]

F. P. Walters in his masterful history of the League of Na-

[13] *The Quest for Peace,* 136.
[14] *International Relations as Viewed from Geneva,* 143.
[15] *The Geneva Experiment,* 107.
[16] Grace E. Rhoads, "Amendments of the Covenant of the League of Nations Adopted and Proposed," 192.
[17] *Where Are We Heading?,* 76.

tions stated, "The abandonment of the League by the United States was a blow whose effects can hardly be over-estimated."[18] Nevertheless, he explained, the other Allied governments thought the League might prove valuable and effective, and ought to be given a trial.

The opinions just quoted are sufficient to bring out the fact that competent observers, writing from different points of view and with no disposition to excuse or gloss over the mistakes of American policy, were inclined to agree that the effect of rejection by the United States was serious but not necessarily fatal.[19] They did not say that the United States killed the League, but rather they commented in terms of reduced vitality and lowered life expectancy. They did not speak of a death warrant, but used terms like obstruction, inhibition, a major reason for failure, a serious blow.

Other evidence exists for the view that rejection by the United States was serious but not fatal. For one thing, the League did operate without American membership for twenty years, and it did achieve some successes, especially in the first ten years of its existence. In addition to its accomplishments in the nonpolitical field the League had considerably influence in settling a number of disputes during that period.[20] Strangely enough, the League had its greatest successes in the control of international conflict during the years when the United States was the least co-operative. This is, of course, a coincidence in chronology and not a significant correlation. There were many other reasons for the League's ability to handle comparatively minor disputes during the 1920's and its failure to halt vastly more serious aggression by major powers during the 1930's. The disputes which were settled without American participa-

18 *A History of the League of Nations*, I, 72.

19 One highly competent account of the League of Nations leaned somewhat to the optimistic side at this point by seeing some advantage to Europe in the nonmembership of the United States. "The result has proved that the co-operation of the United States was not necessary to the success of the League nor to the safety of Europe." John S. Bassett, *The League of Nations: A Chapter in World Politics*, 32.

20 See Conwell-Evans, *The League Council in Action;* Burton, *The Assembly of the League of Nations.*

tion or co-operation were those in which such assistance was not necessary in the premises. Nevertheless, it remains true that the League could and did function to some extent without the United States.

Another consideration lies in the fact that membership in itself is no guarantee of co-operation or of success. Lack of co-operation can be shown within an organization. The attitude of the United States toward joining the League did not of itself make the difference between failure and success of the latter because, if for no other reason, membership would not have assured success. It would certainly be a fallacy to argue that rejection by the United States was solely responsible for the failure, since such an argument would imply the assumption that no other significant causes of failure existed. A comparison of attitudes of various states toward the League might be helpful at this point. The United States never joined but showed some willingness to co-operate after 1928. Germany joined in 1926 but gave notice of withdrawal[21] in 1933 and from then on openly defied the League. Japan was an original member but precipitated a cycle of aggression in 1931. The U.S.S.R. joined in 1934, but the co-operation between the Soviets and the other members was far from wholehearted, and the U.S.S.R. achieved the distinction of being the only state ever expelled from the League. As a matter of fact, there was a time when some members of the League showed a willingness to turn a nonmember (Germany) against a fellow member (the U.S.S.R.) for their own conception of their national interests. Finally, Great Britain and France, leading members of the League from the beginning, had their moments of appeasement, which certainly went further in weakening collective security than absolutely required by any apprehensions about the position of the United States.

The nonmember of next importance to the United States was the U.S.S.R. Here again there was a limitation of geographic inclusiveness, leaving a large gap indeed, the implications of

---

[21] Under Article 1, paragraph 3, a member might withdraw by giving two years' notice of intention, provided all its obligations were fulfilled.

which went beyond geographic incompleteness to an important effect on the attitudes and policies of the League members. The early attitude of the Soviet Union toward the League of Nations is concisely set forth in the following paragraph:

> The attitude of the Soviet Government to the so-called League of Nations has frequently been expressed in the declarations of its responsible representatives. The Soviet Government's attitude to the so-called League of Nations remains unaltered. It regards it as a coalition of certain States, endeavouring to usurp the power over other States and masking their attempts on the rights and independence of other nations by a false appearance of groundless legality and in the form of the mandates issued by the Council or . . . Assembly of the League of Nations, etc. The Soviet Government maintains its conviction that this pseudo-international body really serves as a mere mask to conceal from the broad masses the aggressive aims of the imperialist policy of certain Great Powers or their vassals. The Soviet Government finds confirmation for its convictions every time that a State assuming the leading role in the League of Nations makes a decision on international questions, touching the interests of the Soviet Republic.[22]

Presumably this attitude was overcome or at least muffled, as the U.S.S.R. later became a member of the League, made contributions of some importance to discussions of collective security, and in the disarmament conferences repeatedly suggested that the way to disarm was to disarm. This collaboration between Moscow and Geneva was comparatively short-lived, however, ending with expulsion of the Soviet Union for aggression against Finland. Even during the most co-operative period, furthermore, more than a modicum of mutual suspicion existed between the Soviets and the Western democracies. Undoubtedly apprehension in London and Paris over a westward expansion of communism played its role in the reluctance to take severe measures against the fascist governments which had come to power in the main buffer zone against that expansion. Sanctions which toppled the governments of Italy

---

[22] From "Appendix A—Consent of Government of R.S.F.S.R. to Attend Conference on Reduction of Naval Armaments. Note Sent by People's Commissariat for Foreign Affairs to General Secretary of League of Nations, March 15th, 1923." Quoted by Marina Salvin, "Soviet Policy Toward Disarmament," 60.

and Germany might open those countries to the inroads of communism. The suspicion which stood in the way of effective collaboration was well stated by Sumner Welles in these words:

> The reasons the Allied powers failed to make of their victory a lasting settlement of the German problem, embodying the real ends for which the war had been fought, became ever more clear as the years passed. These reasons can be very simply set forth.
>
> In the first place, the Soviet Union remained outside the family of nations. The Allied powers regarded her as a dangerous menace in international affairs. Some of the powers, notably Great Britain and France, considered her an even greater danger to their security, in the troubled social conditions which arose after the war years, than Germany herself. The Soviet Union undertook to flirt with the Weimar government, thus giving the Western powers a severe attack of nerves, and thereby making it less likely that any continuing form of Western pressure would be brought to bear upon the Soviet Union.[23]

Thus, to the concern lest the application of sanctions incur the wrath of a friend was added the fear that they might also result in strengthening a hostile power. To risk opposition from the United States and to take a chance on the extension of Soviet influence into eastern and central Europe would have been serious business for the leadership of France and Great Britain.

Only one other Great Power—Germany—was outside the League of Nations at its inception. This particular limitation on full acceptance of the principle of concern was of comparatively little significance, provided only that this gap be filled as the defeated nations found their way back into full participation in international affairs. Germany became a member of the League in 1926. It was not in the first years of that organization, but later, that the attitude of Germany became a really serious obstacle to its success.

[23] Welles, 75.

2. Limitation by Interpretation

Another way in which acceptance of the principle of concern was limited lay in a series of interpretations adopted for the guidance of the League. These interpretations were directed at Article 16, which provided for sanctions in the event that a member of the League should take up arms contrary to its obligations for pacific settlement under the Covenant. The first paragraph of Article 16 read:

Should any Member of the League resort to war in disregard of its covenants under Articles 12, 13 or 15, it shall *ipso facto* be deemed to have committed an act of war against all other members of the League, which hereby undertake immediately to subject it to the severance of all trade or financial relations, the prohibition of all intercourse between their nationals and the nationals of the covenant-breaking State, and the prevention of all financial, commercial or personal intercourse between the nationals of the covenant-breaking State and the nationals of any other State, whether a Member of the League or not.

This language had to be interpreted for two reasons: (a) the lack of procedural machinery for determining when a state had resorted to war in violation of the Covenant and (b) the difficulty of carrying out completely the sanctions stipulated by Article 16. There was a recoil from these drastic provisions as some of their implications became more obvious and as it became clear that the League was not to be a universal institution.

The first major attempt to interpret the obligations of Article 16 was made by the International Blockade Committee, which submitted its report in 1921. The work of this committee and consideration of its recommendations resulted in three basic interpretative principles,[24] which remained the official guiding rules of the League. They were:

[24] League of Nations, *Official Journal,* 1920, 1921, 1922; *The Records of the First Assembly,* Meetings of the Committees, II, 261-70, 329-39, Plenary Meetings, 392-410; *The Records of the Second Assembly,* Meetings of the Committees, I, 355-58, Plenary Meetings, 425 ff.; *Reports and Resolutions on the Subject of Article 16 of the Covenant.*

(1) Each member of the League should decide for itself the applicability of sanctions. Obviously the enforcement measures of Article 16 had to come into use either automatically as the result of a violation by a member of the League, by decision of the Council, or by decisions of the other members. Automatic application was rejected early, in fact in the drafting of the Covenant. The so-called Phillimore draft had provided, "If . . . one of the Allied States should break the covenant . . . this State will become *ipso facto* at war with all the other Allied States." It was pointed out that this language would violate the constitution of the United States, providing for the declaration of war by Congress.[25] The final language of Article 16 provided that the covenant-breaking state "shall *ipso facto* be deemed to have committed an act of war against all other members of the League." There was, of course, no language in the final form of Article 16 to bar the automatic application of sanctions as the result of such an act of war. However, recognition of the need for procedural machinery was sufficient to destroy any possibility of purely automatic application. Furthermore, to treat sanctions as automatic would give a violator of the Covenant the power to throw other members of the League into a state of war.

If the action of a violating state did not *ipso facto* give rise to the application of sanctions, it followed that either some organ of the League or the individual members themselves must be vested with the responsibility of making the decision. The official interpretations of Article 16 rejected the former possibility and left the determination to the individual members.

(2) The application of sanctions might be gradual and partial, rather than immediate and complete. It was felt that the provisions of Article 16 were too drastic, if taken literally, to be enforced. Therefore, the International Blockade Committee recommended only the measures which "would most closely accord with the facts of the situation." Sanctions were con-

[25] Miller, II, 80.

sidered to be essentially economic in character; only such measures needed to be taken as would be calculated to exercise a decisive influence on the economic resisting power of the defaulting state. The word "immediately" was taken to mean "at the earliest possible moment at which unanimous action could be secured." It meant that a breach of the Covenant would give rise to an immediate obligation to take the appropriate measures, but not necessarily an obligation to take them immediately.[26]

(3) The "peculiar position" of each state might be taken into consideration. Switzerland insisted on safeguarding its traditional neutrality; Denmark, Norway, and Sweden proposed to amend Article 16 so that a member of the League for whom the application of sanctions "might entail serious danger" could be authorized by the Council to maintain certain relations with a Covenant-breaking state; a Canadian memorandum expressed objections to measures likely to divert the markets of members of the League to competitors free of the onerous obligations of Article 16. The International Blockade Committee recognized that the granting of certain exceptions might be required, since "it is possible to imagine cases in which the full application by some State of the financial and commercial measures laid down would create such hardships and dangers as to be almost intolerable."[27] In connection with a consideration of the amendments to the Covenant proposed by the Scandinavian governments the committee suggested that Article 16 should be amended by the addition of the following sentence: "The Council may, however, at the request of a Member which can show that the facilities demanded are essential for its economic or political security, grant such exemptions as in its opinion will not conflict with the aims of Article 16."[28]

Thus, the principle of concern was limited through interpre-

[26] League of Nations, *The Records of the Second Assembly*, Plenary Meetings, 431.
[27] League of Nations, *Reports and Resolutions*, 19.
[28] Same, 19-20.

tations of the obligations undertaken. Instead of the crucial determination of a violation of the Covenant being placed with an organ of the entire group, the individual members were left free to make their own decisions. Instead of immediate and complete application of sanctions, the measures would be taken on a gradual and partial basis. Instead of full participation by all members of the League (and co-operating non-members), some might be excused on account of their "peculiar position." This was indeed a limitation on general acceptance.

The limitations arrived at by interpretations of Article 16 during 1920-1921 resulted from a compromise of the maximum view of collective sanctions against a violator of the Covenant, that controls over international conflict should be centralized in some organ or agency of the entire League. Since the Council of the League had the major responsibility for enforcing the peace, the problem became one of the extent of the Council's effective authority. International solidarity in the face of a breach of the peace was an essential postulate of the entire League system. This could not be maintained without some centralization of decisions and co-ordination of measures to effect the decisions. From this point of view the interpretations of 1920-1921 limited the principle of concern and thereby weakened the League even more than appeared from the statements and resolutions themselves.

The compromise finally accepted was based on the first of the principles set forth by the International Blockade Committee. The resolution adopted by the First Assembly provided in substance that each member would be the final judge of an occasion for sanctions, but that its duty to take the measures envisaged by Article 16 would follow automatically from recognition of such an occasion. The resolutions concerning the procedure for notification and application of sanctions tended to convey the impression that a decision by individual members would be followed by co-ordinated action taken by all according to certain standard criteria. However, a close examination of the language used shows that nothing was really left to control by the Council as a centralizing authority. The

Council's opinion would be sent to all members of the League with a statement of reasons and "an invitation to take action accordingly." The Council would "recommend the date on which the enforcement of economic pressure, under Article 16, is to be begun, and shall give notice of that date to all the Members of the League." It would suggest a plan for joint action on the various economic, commercial, and financial measures to be taken. All members would be treated alike in the application of the measures with certain stipulated exceptions, but the resolutions were silent on the question of authority to pass on the validity of exceptions which might be sought by the members. Thus, even in the application of sanctions after the appropriate decision had been made, the Council could only recommend, invite, and notify. The interpretative resolutions carefully refrained from saying that the Council directed anything. The way was left open for the individual members to decide for themselves not only if sanctions would be applied, but when, how, and to what extent.

The interpretations of 1921 were adopted as provisional measures pending the amendment of Article 16 as proposed by the Assembly resolutions. It was expected that the interim governed by provisional interpretations would be comparatively short. Constitutional recognition that the text of Article 16 was too stringent for practical application seemed to be in order. However, the proposed amendments did not secure the required number of ratifications, and the original text of Article 16 remained officially in force. Yet limitation by interpretation was not a passing phase, with general acceptance of the principle of concern renewed by failure of the proposed amendments. The limiting interpretations prevailed despite the continuance of the original text. Confirmation of this fact is found in an examination of a later series of interpretaions during the period 1926-1928.[29]

The question of interpreting the principle of concern in relation to the League of Nations arose also in connection with the

[29] For the interpretations used in connection with the practical application of sanctions, see Chapter V, section 1.

work of the Preparatory Commission for the Disarmament Conference. A French proposal raised two questions:

1. "On what principles will it be possible to draw up a scale of armaments permissible to the various countries, taking into account . . . the degree of security which, in the event of aggression, a State could receive under the provisions of the Covenant or of separate engagements contracted towards that State?"

2. "Can the reduction of armaments be promoted by examining possible means for ensuring that the mutual assistance, economic and military, contemplated in Article 16 of the Covenant shall be brought quickly into operation as soon as an act of aggression has been committed?"[30]

On the basis of these questions there was referred to a committee of the Council the consideration of the methods or regulations which would "enable the Council to take such decisions as may be necessary to enforce the obligations of the Covenant as expeditiously as possible." This committee based its discussion of this problem upon a report[31] submitted at its request by de Brouckère of Belgium.

The embarrassment at the situation with respect to the limiting interpretations, their acceptance in fact but not by constitutional process, is well shown by the following statements in the de Brouckère report:

The starting-point had been Article 16 as drafted by the authors of the Covenant, and an endeavour had been made to determine the most satisfactory rules for its application. Certain rules had then been conceived the effect of which should, in the mind of those responsible for them, have been most satisfactory, but which were not entirely consistent with part of the text. An endeavour was then made to obviate this difficulty by a system of interpretation which was in certain cases somewhat bold. It had then been decided that the best solution of the difficulty was to modify Article 16 itself by means of amendments referring to various provisions of that article. The result was that, after having sought to find rules to fit the text, an attempt was finally made to find a text to fit the rules.[32]

[30] League of Nations, *Reports and Resolutions*, 61.
[31] For text, see same, 60-72.   [32] Same, 62.

The de Brouckère report recognized the crucial importance of the question, Whose duty was it to decide whether sanctions were applicable? Not every act of international violence would give rise to an occasion for action. For example, an unintentional and clearly insignificant violation of a remote colonial frontier would not justify the invocation of Article 16. Any measures taken must be proportionate to the seriousness of the attack and justified by the imminence of the danger. This involved the concept of "legitimate defense." A country which flagrantly exceeded the bounds of legitimate defense would be the real aggressor. Accordingly the determination of a "resort to war" under Article 16 might not always be clear, obvious, and easy. This enhanced the importance of the locus of authority to make the controlling decision. On this point the report unhesitatingly followed the interpretations of 1921 and affirmed that the Covenant allowed only one reply to be given—each member must decide for itself. However, some qualification was placed on this interpretation by stating that the duty of each member to decide did not leave it free to make any arbitrary decision whatsoever. Refusal to apply sanctions in an obvious case of aggression would be a violation of the Covenant and might lead to expulsion from the League. Furthermore, if a member took advantage of false allegations that another state had resorted to war, it might well become the object of sanctions itself.

The other two leading principles of interpretation—that sanctions might be gradual and partial and that the peculiar position of individual members might be taken into account—the de Brouckère report considered incompatible with the text of the Covenant. It pointed out that the question of gradual, partial, and incomplete application of sanctions would lose much of its importance if recourse to Article 16 was understood as a last desperate measure after all attempts to conserve peace had failed. If war should occur, delay in taking action against the aggressor could only result in retarding the restoration of peace. In this connection the report stated:

Article 16 deals with a contingency to be dreaded. It lays down terrible measures for the extreme case in which the pacific endeavours of the League finally fail before the criminal determination of a State resolved on war. Recourse to this article, except where absolutely necessary, would embitter conflicts instead of allaying them. It would, moreover, be extremely unfortunate to appeal to it in vain when the intention is not to apply it or to make but a show of applying it. To say that ambassadors only will be recalled under an article which definitely requires the breaking-off of all personal relations; to say that certain commercial relations will be gradually severed when the text demands that they should *all* be broken off *forthwith* is to make an almost ridiculous use of a clause in which the peoples most exposed to aggression see their supreme safeguard. It means weakening it dangerously and at the same time weakening the whole League.[33]

One other point of interest in connection with the de Brouckère report is its recognition that control over the decision to apply sanctions implied control over the measures taken in their application. "Since it is the States which, from a strictly legal point of view, are empowered to decide whether sanctions should be applied, it seems to follow that they alone are qualified to control them in practice." The Council would make recommendations "to ensure concerted and effective action," but actual control of armed forces would remain with the members themselves and economic sanctions would be applied "by the various States on similar lines."[34]

Another study of the problem of sanctions is found in a report, submitted to the Council of the League in June, 1927, by the Secretary-General, on the subject of "the legal position which would be brought about by enforcing in time of peace the measures of economic pressure indicated in Article 16 of the Covenant, particularly by a maritime blockade."[35] This report was concerned with the legal situation arising from the application of Article 16 rather than with an interpretation of its provisions with respect to the extent of the obligations resting upon the members of the League. However, the report

[33] Same, 70.   [34] Same, 73.
[35] Text in same, 83-88. See also League of Nations, *Official Journal,* 1927, pp. 834-39.

accepted the interpretation of 1921 but "assumed that any application of the article would in fact be preceded and controlled by recommendations of the Council and that it would be a misapplication of the article, which would not be tolerated, if a Member or group of Members should claim to act under it on their own account in defiance of the general sentiment of the League."[36]

The report distinguished the legal position of a League member applying sanctions with respect to (a) the Covenant-breaking state, (b) other members of the League, and (c) third states. For the first of these the Covenant was held to provide a basis for the legality of adverse differential treatment of an aggressor, whether or not a state of war was recognized to exist. With reference to the second type of situation, relating to the other members of the League, it was obvious under the interpretative resolutions that it would be possible for some members to decide that sanctions were applicable in a given case and for other members to disagree. In this situation would a member deciding not to apply sanctions be bound to recognize that other members had a right to make an affirmative decision, even though the interests of the former might be adversely affected? Or would the attitude of each member be guided solely by its own opinion as to the occasion for sanctions? In this dilemma the view taken by the Secretary-General was stated as follows:

Although the matter is not free from doubt, the better view appears to be that the Member, while entitled to decide for itself if there has been a breach of the Covenant which justifies and obliges it to apply Article 16, is bound as a party to the article to recognise the right of the other Members to hold for their part that there has been a breach of the Covenant and to interrupt intercourse with the peccant State and the nationals and territory of all other States, including those of the Member itself. . . . Its position is in fact one for which express provision is not made in Article 16, which appears to be inspired by the hope that the Members of the League will in fact be unanimous.[37]

[36] League of Nations, *Official Journal*, 1927, p. 834.
[37] Same, 836.

The last type of situation, with reference to third states, was considered as the one giving rise to the most delicate legal questions. The opinion expressed was that third states had no treaty obligation to acquiesce in the measures taken under Article 16, that they had rights under international law that prudently must be respected, and that hopefully they would take a benevolent attitude toward a defensive alliance acting in the sole interest of enforcing the pacific settlement of international disputes.

The studies were continued under the auspices of the Preparatory Commission for the Disarmament Conference and of its Committee on Arbitration and Security. A "Memorandum on Articles 10, 11, and 16 of the Covenant"[38] was submitted to the committee early in 1928 by Rutgers of the Netherlands. This memorandum also took note of the anomalous situation created by the fact that the provisional interpretative resolutions of 1921 had not found support in ratification of the amendments on which they were based. This uncertain situation was considered unsatisfactory, and it was recommended that the proposed amendments either be ratified or finally abandoned.

The mandate of the Committee on Arbitration and Security was to explore the possibilities of the Covenant without changing the obligations of members of the League and without making any attempt at interpretation. Nevertheless, the Rutgers memorandum reflected the acceptance of the earlier interpretations of Article 16. It agreed that each member of the League must decide for itself when a breach of the Covenant has been committed, and continued:

This doctrine is generally accepted today, and even if it were not the Council could not invoke a text or apply a sanction to oblige a Member to obey a decision of the Council in virtue of Article 16 which that Member did not consider to be well founded. It is the Members themselves who must decide on the performance of their obligations under Article 16. It must therefore be realised that when they are called upon to take this extremely grave decision

[38] For text, see same, 1928, pp. 670-86.

they will be guided by their own conception of their obligations under Article 16.

We may go even further than this. If ever the question of the application of Article 16 arose, the decision of the different countries would not depend upon interpretations, however authoritative, or on the deductions of lawyers; the great question would be whether the principle of Article 16 was or was not a living reality. To carry out the grave obligations contained in Article 16, States would have to be inspired by the spirit of responsibility and solidarity which is at the root of Article 16 and of the whole League of Nations.[39]

This memorandum also recognized that the control of the application of sanctions would rest with the individual members, stating: "It is not the Council which has the last word on the measures to be taken in the execution of Article 16. It is for the Members, bearing constantly in mind their duty, to enforce respect for the Covenant, to decide upon what measures they can take. To deal effectively with the aggressor, co-operation is essential. It is clear that, for this co-operation to succeed, it is most desirable that States should have the guidance, in regard to the general situation, of a weighty and authoritative opinion."[40]

The conclusion to be drawn from the discussions of Article 16 during the period 1926-1928 is that the trend toward limitation by interpretation was confirmed. The crucial issue of the controlling decisions was left on exactly the same basis as before, that each member must decide for itself. Even where some of the resolutions of 1921 were criticized or their unsatisfactory results alluded to, there was no escape from the fact that these same resolutions had been officially adopted by both the Assembly and the Council, even though provisionally.

No action ever was taken to rescind the interpretations of 1921 as guiding rules of League action. As a matter of fact the deliberations of 1926-1928 took place immediately upon the heels of a definite indication that the League would be guided by these very interpretations. Germany became a member of the League in 1926. During the preceding negotiations

[39] Same, 679. Paragraph numbering omitted from quotation.
[40] Same, 680.

the German delegates raised questions about obligations under Article 16 and claimed special recognition for Germany's status as a disarmed power.[41] The reply by the Council (March, 1925) was based upon the concept that the occasion for sanctions would be decided by the individual members of the League, but that a decision to apply sanctions would introduce a binding obligation on all members to participate in the measures. After stating that with respect to military forces the Council would make recommendations and Germany then would decide to what extent she was in a position to comply, the reply continued:

As regards economic measures, the States Members of the League themselves decide, either separately or by prior agreement, the practical steps to be taken for the execution of the general obligation which they have undertaken. But the provisions of the Covenant do not permit that, when action is undertaken in pursuance of Article 16, each Member of the League should decide separately whether it shall take any part in that action. The Council feels bound to express its clear opinion that any reservation of this kind would undermine the basis of the League of Nations and would be incompatible with membership of the League. It seems to the Council impossible that a Member of the League, and of the Council, should, in the event of operations undertaken against a covenant-breaking State, retain a status which would exempt its nationals from the general obligations imposed by the Covenant.[42]

This might seem to give the Council somewhat more control than contemplated by the interpretative resolutions of 1921. However, the force of the Council's position was blunted to some extent by another statement made in connection with Germany's entrance into the League. In their collective note dated December 1, 1925, the Locarno Powers indicated their interpretation that each member of the League "is bound to co-operate loyally and effectively in support of the Covenant and in resistance to any act of aggression *to the extent which is compatible with its military situation and takes its geographical position into account.*"[43] Furthermore, in an exchange of notes

---

[41] Same, 1925, pp. 323-26.   [42] Same, 490-91.
[43] League of Nations, *Treaty Series*, 54:299, 301. Italics supplied.

after signature of a treaty of friendship and neutrality between Germany and the U.S.S.R. in 1926, the German government stated that the question of sanctions against the U.S.S.R. could be determined for Germany with binding force only by her own consent.[44]

Thus the official interpretations by the League itself and the understanding by which Germany became a member of the League placed limitations upon the obligations of collective security.

One more bit of evidence may be added to this record of limitation by interpretation, namely, the debates on a proposed amendment of Article 10.[45] This question was raised originally by Canada at the First Assembly in the form of a proposal for the complete elimination of the article. The absence of the United States obviously put Canada in a hazardous position if enforcement measures ever were taken by the League. Also, there was considerable sentiment to the effect that the League was an instrument of European power politics in which Canada had no interest.[46] After discussions at the First and Second Assemblies Canada submitted a new proposal to the Third Assembly that (a) the political and geographic circumstances of each state be taken into consideration and (b) the opinion of the Council should be regarded as of highest importance but not necessarily obligatory. The Third Assembly deferred the discussion, leaving it to the Council to provide for the detailed study of the proposal. The Council decided to invite the views of the members of the League.

The replies were received and the matter was again considered in 1923. After long discussion in committee and before

[44] Same, 53:395.

[45] League of Nations, *Records of the Fourth Assembly*, Plenary Meetings, 75-87, 190-91; Minutes of the First Committee, 11-18, 24-28, 43-53. Article 10 provided: "The Members of the League undertake to respect and preserve as against external aggression the territorial integrity and existing political independence of all members of the League. In case of any such aggression or in case of any threat or danger of such aggression, the Council shall advise upon the means by which this obligation shall be fulfilled."

[46] See, for example, statements by F. H. Underhill and T. W. L. MacDermot, in Maurice Bourquin (ed.), *Collective Security: A Record of the Seventh and Eighth International Studies Conferences*, 49-54.

the full Assembly, a vote was taken on the following interpretative resolution:

The Assembly,
Desirous of defining the scope of the obligations contained in
Article 10 of the Covenant so far as regards the points raised by
the delegation of Canada, adopts the following resolution:
It is in conformity with the spirit of Article 10 that, in the event
of the Council considering it to be its duty to recommend the application of military measures in consequence of an aggression or
danger or threat of aggression, the Council shall be bound to take
account, more particularly, of the geographical situation and of the
special conditions of each State.
It is for the constitutional authorities of each Member to decide,
in reference to the obligation of preserving the independence and
the integrity of the territory of Members, in what degree the Member is bound to assure the execution of this obligation by employment of its military forces;
The recommendation made by the Council shall be regarded as
being of the highest importance, and shall be taken into consideration by all the Members of the League with the desire to execute
their engagements in good faith.[47]

The result is interesting. Twenty-nine states, including all
the Great Powers then members of the League, voted for the
resolution; twenty-two nations were absent or abstained from
voting; and one country, Persia, voted in the negative, explaining that the full guarantee was necessary for a small country
surrounded by nonmembers of the League like Russia, Turkey,
and Afghanistan. The interpretative resolution on Article 10,
thus failing of unanimity, was not adopted. However, the
whole discussion on this matter indicated an overwhelming
sentiment for limiting the force of the article. This sentiment
could not fail to have its effect, even though the wording of the
Covenant remained as before.

[47] League of Nations, *Records of the Fourth Assembly*, Plenary Meetings, 86.

3. The Principle of Traditional Neutrality

Coincident with the incorporation of the principle of concern into international law and organization there was also manifested some dependence upon the principle of traditional neutrality. It is obvious, of course, that refusal on the part of a state to become a member of the League of Nations was a rejection of the principle upon which the League was based, and if such a nation did not in some other way accept the principle of concern, either explicitly or implicitly, it would presumably remain attached to the principle of traditional neutrality. In addition to this situation involving nonmembers, there were some positive survivals of the concept of neutrality.

Switzerland, because its people were convinced that their national welfare demanded the continuance of a status of neutrality (which had been recognized by Article 435 of the Treaty of Versailles), was admitted to the League of Nations by a Council resolution recognizing the unique position of that country and its status of perpetual neutrality. For its part, Switzerland recognized the duties of solidarity imposed by membership in the League. It was understood that the Swiss government would not consider the presence in Geneva of a military commission acting under the authority of the League as incompatible with Swiss neutrality, and a representative of Switzerland went so far as to state before the Assembly, "Switzerland intends to remain neutral from the military point of view, but she does not deny the duty she owes to economic solidarity. She is prepared, if called upon, to bring the economic weapon into play against an enemy of the human race; but on conditions compatible with the conception of neutrality recognized as applying to Switzerland."[48]

[48] League of Nations, *The Records of the First Assembly*, Plenary Meetings, 398. A concise statement of the understandings accompanying Swiss entry into the League may be found in Manley O. Hudson, "Membership in the League of Nations," *American Journal of International Law*, XVIII (1924), 439, 440, and notes. For a brief discussion of the dilemma of Switzerland with regard to military neutrality and economic sanctions, see Walter H. Zahler, "Switzerland

During the Greco-Turkish War the Allied governments issued, in 1921, a collective declaration of neutrality, when Greece was a member of the League and Turkey was not.

The Nine-Power Treaty concluded at the Washington Conference of 1922 between the United States and eight members of the League having interests in the Far East contained a provision to the effect that China's rights as a neutral in time of war "to which China is not a party" would be respected.

In the decade after the adoption of the Covenant several bilateral neutrality treaties were signed by various members of the League. Probably the most important development with regard to this type of treaty was its use as an essential element in the security system of the U.S.S.R. The restoration of peace between the Soviet republics and adjacent countries was accompanied by a series of treaties designed to prevent the recurrence of wars (especially attacks by "capitalist" nations upon the communist society) by means of recognition of the independence of the newly created boundary states, reciprocal guarantees against future attacks, acceptance of the principle of nonintervention, and an assumption of a policy of neutrality by signatories toward each other in the event of hostilities.[49]

Immediately after the adoption of the Treaties of Locarno in 1925 the U.S.S.R. concluded with Turkey the first of a series of bilateral mutual security treaties which accepted the principle of neutrality.[50] This was followed in April, 1926, by a treaty between the U.S.S.R. and Germany which provided (Article 2) that "should one of the Contracting Parties, despite its peaceful attitude, be attacked by one or more third Powers,

and the League of Nations," 753-57. In the case of Belgium the neutralization treaties of 1839 were abrogated by Article 31 of the Treaty of Versailles, and Belgium became a member of the League without any recognition that its position was "unique." For the status of Belgium, see Harold J. Tobin, "Is Belgium Still Neutralized?" American Journal of International Law, XXVI (1932), 514-32. In 1936, however, Belgium insisted on a right to remain neutral in the event of war, adopting a policy aimed "solely . . . at placing us outside the quarrels of our neighbors and keeping war from our territory."

[49] Malbone W. Graham, Jr., "The Soviet Security Treaties," American Journal of International Law, XXIII (1929), 336. For the Soviet security policies, see T. A. Taracouzio, The Soviet Union and International Law.

[50] Graham, 339.

the other Contracting Party shall observe neutrality for the whole duration of the conflict."[51]

In a note of the same date the German government declared that there could be no conflict between the provisions of this treaty and the entry of Germany into the League of Nations, since the application of sanctions against the U.S.S.R. under Article 16 of the Covenant would come into consideration only if that state should enter upon a war of aggression, and the question of whether the U.S.S.R. had committed such an aggression could be determined for Germany only by her own consent. With reference to the question of whether and to what extent Germany "would be in a position to take part in the application of sanctions," attention was called to the note of interpretation of Article 16 addressed to the German representatives on the occasion of the signing of the Treaties of Locarno.[52] The government of the U.S.S.R. "took note of" these explanations without further comment.

A treaty of nonaggression between the U.S.S.R. and Lithuania, signed September 28, 1926, while not using the term "neutrality" in the treaty itself, provided by Article 3 that "each of the two Contracting Parties undertakes to refrain from any act of aggression whatsoever against the other Party. Should one of the Contracting Parties, despite its peaceful attitude, be attacked by one or several third Powers, the other Contracting Party undertakes not to support the said third Power against the Contracting Party attacked."[53]

In an exchange of notes the Lithuanian government declared that Lithuania's membership in the League of Nations could not constitute an obstacle to friendly relations with the U.S.S.R. and that in view of Lithuania's geographical position the obligations of League membership "cannot constitute an obstacle to the Lithuanian nation's aspirations towards neutrality, which is the policy best suited to her vital interests."[54]

Finally, a treaty of guarantee and neutrality between Persia

[51] League of Nations, *Treaty Series*, 53:393. [52] Same, 393-96.
[53] Same, 60:153. This treaty was renewed on May 6, 1931 (same, 125:255-63).
[54] Same, 60:155-57.

and the U.S.S.R., signed October 1, 1927, contained a pledge of neutrality binding on the victim of aggression as well as its cosignatory: "Should either of the Contracting Parties become the victim of aggression on the part of one or more third Powers, the other Contracting Party agrees to observe neutrality throughout the duration of the conflict, while the Party which is the victim of aggression shall not violate that neutrality, notwithstanding any strategical, tactical, or political considerations or any advantages it might thereby obtain."[55]

Another aspect of the principle of traditional neutrality related to the formulation of belligerent and neutral rights and duties in time of war. The controversies over neutral rights and duties which had arisen between Great Britain and the United States from 1914 to 1917 had been left for later adjustment, and the claims and counterclaims were settled by an exchange of notes of May 10, 1927. This settlement definitely abandoned any attempt on the part of the United States government to ascertain the validity of claims against Great Britain for violating neutral rights. Furthermore, no regulation for the future was adopted, it being provided "that the right of each Government to maintain in the future such position as it may deem appropriate with respect to the legality or illegality under international law of measures such as those giving rise to claims covered by the immediately preceding paragraph is fully reserved, it being specifically understood that the juridical position of neither Government is prejudiced by the present agreement."[56]

The Havana Convention on Maritime Neutrality, signed in 1928, formulated the rights and duties of neutrals in time of war, but it was ratified only by the United States and a few of the smaller Latin American countries. The several multilateral treaties for the regulation of certain facilities and utilities of international concern (such as navigable waterways and commercial aviation) did not undertake to define neutral

[55] Same, 112:292. Persia was a member of the League at the time.
[56] Article 1, section 3, United States Department of State, *Treaty Series*, No. 756, pp. 1, 4.

and belligerent rights and obligations in time of war. Although the problem of restating or clarifying the status of the law of neutrality was recognized early in the history of the League, the work of various committees of jurists, both official and unofficial, did not result in the formulation of any generally accepted code.

Any dependence upon traditional neutrality raises the problem of the relation of that principle to the development of a system based upon differential treatment. An interpretation of the implications of continued acceptance of the nineteenth century conception in any form must logically either construe the two alternatives as definitely exclusive of each other or posit the assumption that certain aspects of the earlier system will function as transitional elements in the establishment and integration of a system of collective security. The so-called "neutrality treaties" furnish an apt instance of this problem. There has been no occasion for a court of competent jurisdiction to pronounce upon the rights and duties flowing from these treaties, and therefore no authoritative opinion of their juridical import is available. Clearly, nevertheless, to interpret the neutrality treaties as requiring impartiality left—so far as League members were concerned—the possibility of conflict with the obligations of Article 16. However, a promise to remain neutral might be interpreted as superseded by the obligations of Article 16, provided a cosignatory were found to be a victim of aggression. According to such an interpretation the neutrality treaties would be supplementary to the peace system of the Covenant. On the other hand, the obligations of a neutrality treaty combined with the accepted interpretation that each state might decide its own participation in sanctions obviously might operate to impede the functioning of a collective system.

The problem of interpreting the significance of the neutrality treaties was merely one instance of confusion with respect to international law and organization for the restraint of violence among states. The partial acceptance of the principle of concern and the uncertain position of neutrality meant the coexistence of two antithetical principles, neither of which was accorded the support requisite to its functioning as a dependable instrument for the control of international violence. Neutrality, as well as collective security, contemplates the existence of an international system. The control or restriction of international violence absolutely requires the regularization of the relations of third states with nations involved in hostilities. When two juridical systems compete with each other within the same area of social organization the result is likely to be their mutual destruction. This is true because the very existence of law depends upon the "security of expectation." When customary law is no longer observed and no law by agreement takes its place, there is no positive basis for that general acquiescence essential to law. Whenever unregulated violence, in the form of undeclared wars and coercive diplomacy, occurs, the essential relevance of *any* international juridical system is denied.

4. Disarmament, Security, Arbitration

The problem of disarmament is implicit in the problems of war and peace, of international law and organization, of national safety and collective security. To separate the devising of means from the choice of ends is to adopt a false dichotomy and to sever two vitally connected aspects of the same fundamental issue. If war is expected or planned, the weapons of war will not be abandoned. Any willingness to reduce armaments will be the result of a desire to reduce an opponent's armaments still more or a bid for the sanction of moral approbation. On the other hand, if war should become a defunct institution, national armaments would become merely quaint relics of a past era. In fact, under the expectation of peace there would be competition in reduction of armaments.

As it is, desire for peace is reconciled with feverish preparation for war by the argument that lack of preparedness will increase the likelihood of involvement in war. A weak defense is said to invite an offensive attack. But when all states attempt to achieve the strongest possible military defense and when an effective offense is considered the best defense, the armaments which are to guarantee peace may become an important cause of war. To a fortunate few among the states national armaments may bring a more or less permanent security against war, but such a peace will be an interval between wars, and what security there is will be little more than a protracted interruption of active hostilities. Under a genuine system of collective security wars might occur, since "perfect peace" is a figment of the imagination, but they would be no more than unfortunate incidents in an essentially sane world. Each state would not be in momentary expectation of fighting for its existence. The difference between peace by armament and peace by disarmament is the difference between whether a system based upon the ultimate sanction of nationalistic war is to be the normal or the abnormal condition of international relations. It is clear, therefore, that the status of the armaments problem is an excellent test of whether or not the principle of concern is being made functionally effective in international organization.

The Covenant of the League of Nations provided that "the Members of the League recognize that the maintenance of peace requires the reduction of national armaments to the lowest point consistent with national safety and the enforcement by common action of international obligations."[57] A Temporary Mixed Commission was constituted to prepare reports and proposals for the reduction of armaments, and each member of the League was requested to furnish a statement of considerations in this matter. The conclusion which emerged was that under existing conditions the majority of governments would be unable to accept the responsibility for a serious reduction of armaments unless they received in exchange a satisfactory guarantee of the safety of their countries. In other words, the governments expressed willingness to reduce their armaments, but they also emphasized the jeopardy to national

[57] Article 8, paragraph 1.

safety if they did so. Security had to precede disarmament. The Temporary Mixed Commission's report accordingly proposed that the security upon which disarmament depended be achieved by a general defensive agreement requiring immediate and effective assistance to any signatory which might be the object of attack, such an agreement to be conditional on an actual reduction of armaments. There would be discrimination against any state which might "resort to war." Thus the principle of differential treatment was applied to the problem of disarmament.

The Assembly, after considering the report of the Temporary Mixed Commission, adopted a resolution instructing the commission to continue its investigations and to prepare a draft treaty embodying the principle of achieving disarmament as a result of security based on an assurance of mutual assistance.[58] In pursuance of this resolution a draft Treaty of Mutual Assistance was submitted to the Assembly in 1923. Article 1 of the draft treaty provided that "the High Contracting Parties solemnly declare that aggressive war is an international crime and severally undertake that no one of them will be guilty of its commission."

By Article 2 the signatories would undertake, jointly and severally, to "furnish assistance, in accordance with the provisions of the Present Treaty, to any one of their number should the latter be the object of a war of aggression, provided that it has conformed to the provisions of the present Treaty regarding the reduction or limitation of armaments."

The sanctions of the draft treaty were contained in Article 5, by which the signatories would undertake, in case a situation arose under Article 2, to furnish assistance in the form determined by the Council of the League as the most effective and "to take all appropriate measures without delay in the order of urgency demanded by the circumstances." In particular the Council would be authorized to decide to apply

[58] "Resolutions and Recommendations Adopted by the Assembly during Its Third Session," League of Nations, *Official Journal,* Special Supplement No. 9 (October, 1922), 26-27.

immediately to the aggressor state the economic sanctions contemplated by Article 16 of the Covenant, to invoke by name the signatories whose assistance it required,[59] to determine the forces which each nation furnishing assistance should place at its disposal, to prescribe all necessary measures for securing priority for the communications and transport connected with the operations, to prepare a plan of financial cooperation, and to appoint the higher command and establish the object and nature of his duties. Thus the draft treaty provided for an increase of some importance in the authority of the Council, since the latter would be authorized to make the final decisions upon the application of economic and military sanctions.

On September 29, 1923, the Assembly passed a resolution which, after noting that the discussion of the draft treaty had revealed some divergencies of opinion and that a large number of governments had not yet expressed their views, requested the Council "to submit the draft Treaty of Mutual Assistance to the Governments for their consideration, asking them to communicate their views in regard to the aforesaid draft Treaty."[60]

A total of twenty-nine governments, including three non-members of the League,[61] submitted their comments before the meeting of the Fifth Assembly in 1924.[62] The attitude of most of the replies was an acceptance of the draft treaty as a basis for discussion, with more or less strenuous objections to some of its particular provisions. A few states rejected the draft altogether; among them was the United States, which merely noted the more important provisions and stated that it would "find it impossible to give its adherence."[63]

[59] Subject to the provision that no signatory situated in a continent other than that in which operations take place would, in principle, be required to cooperate in military, naval, or air operations.

[60] League of Nations, *Official Journal*, Special Supplement No. 13 (1923); *Records of the Fourth Assembly*, Plenary Meetings, Text of the Debates, 154.

[61] Germany, the United States, and the U.S.S.R.

[62] League of Nations, *Arbitration, Security, and Reduction of Armaments*, 221-60.

[63] Same, 232-34.

Those with specific objections fell into three principal groups.[64] First, the U.S.S.R., Norway, and Sweden refused to accept the principle upon which the draft treaty was based—namely, that the limitation of national armaments should be contingent upon the establishment of an international organization for the prevention of war. Norway pointed out in particular that Article 8 obligated the members of the League to reduce their armaments without guarantees other than those in the Covenant itself.[65]

Second, a large number of objections were based on doubts about the value of such a treaty. Twelve governments contended that the guarantees provided were not sufficient to justify reduction of armaments, or in slightly different words, that the treaty, even if accepted, would not accomplish its purpose. The same point was involved in other references to the probable delays in bringing assistance to a victim of aggression and to the belief that the treaty did not provide security because it would be too easy to denounce. Finland further stated that the signatories would not know how much assistance they could count on when estimating to what extent they could reduce armaments and that it was not clear how mutual assistance was to be organized.

[64] It is necessary to enter the warning that an itemization of the objections to the draft treaty is a relatively crude index of the degree of its acceptance. A given criticism might be presented either as an insuperable obstacle to acceptance of the treaty or as a mildly desirable modification. A government hostile to the treaty might simply state its attitude without specifying a single defect, or it might not reply at all. A suggestion for a change in wording might be made with the intention either of strengthening the treaty or of rendering it practically meaningless by a subterfuge. The real question was not whether any objections were presented, but whether some effective plan could be worked out and adopted within a reasonable length of time. However, the objections presented in the comments of the various governments may be accepted as a reasonably accurate indication of the difficulties involved in working out a system of disarmament by adverse differential treatment of any state which might resort to war.

[65] In answer to the argument that Article 8 required disarmament regardless of any guarantees, it had been held that the interdependence of disarmament and guarantees of security were the result of practical experience, not a legal principle. League of Nations, *Reduction of Armaments*, 3. However, a more defensible position would have been an invocation of the qualifying phrase, "the lowest point consistent with national safety."

Some governments considered that aside from being ineffective, the adoption of the draft treaty would be actually harmful. The Netherlands questioned whether the plan was in accord with the principles of the Covenant, and Norway objected to treaties of guarantee increasing the obligations imposed by the Covenant. Several governments thought an unwise extension of the powers of the Council would be involved, and Sweden objected that the sanctions of the Covenant would be extended without a corresponding extension of rules for the pacific solution of international disputes.

One of the most disputed points was the provision which would permit the conclusion of complementary regional agreements within the framework of the draft treaty. These would ostensibly be designed to supplement the general treaty and increase its effectiveness by the formation of especially strong systems of mutual assistance in regions where the danger of aggression might be acute. However, a revival of the prewar system of hostile alliances was widely feared, and thirteen governments registered their objections to allowing such regional agreements.

The U.S.S.R. contended that under the existing conditions an international organization such as that contemplated by the draft treaty would become an instrument of an aggressive policy by dominant states. Germany took a similar position in stating that the dictates of the Council might involve third states in a war more serious for them than for the original participants; the Netherlands objected that there was no legal guarantee that aid would be extended only to those nations in a position to claim it rightfully. Germany also stated that the draft treaty contained no objective standards for disarmament and concurred with Sweden in the view that a disproportion existed between the burdens and the advantages which would result. Norway made the criticism that there was too much dependence on military strength. Great Britain, Greece, and the Netherlands feared that the net result might even be an increased necessity for armaments.

Another series of objections to the draft treaty based on

doubts about its effectiveness and constructive consequences involved references to the special circumstances of particular states.[66]

Lithuania pointed out that a guarantee to respect territorial integrity presupposes that frontiers have been regularly established and are recognized by the states concerned. This condition was not satisfied with regard to Vilna. Accordingly the Lithuanian government stated that it "could not undertake to come to the assistance of Poland, should the latter be the victim of an act of aggression, unless and until she restores Vilna, the age-long capital of Lithuania, together with the adjacent territory, which Poland now occupies in violation of treaties and of her own international engagements."[67]

Canada felt that her position in the British Empire affected the protection afforded her by the continental limitation of the application of the treaty. Canada had already expressed disapproval of an interpretation of Article 10 of the Covenant which would require her to intervene actively under that article, and it was her view that the proposed treaty created an obligation wider in its extent and more precise in its implications than any which Article 10 could be interpreted as imposing.

Uruguay objected that its geographical location, combined with the difficulty of communications, would leave it in an unprotected position, and therefore the treaty would be useless in promoting that country's national security. Uruguay especially objected to the grouping of the Americas into three continental divisions for the purpose of the treaty, pointing out that so far as military, naval, and air operations were concerned, no state in North or Central America would be obligated to come to the assistance of any South American state.

The Greek government found itself in a "very special position," based on the claims that the territorial status of Greece

[66] One may safely assume that "special circumstances of particular states" were not forgotten in the formulation of general objections to the draft Treaty of Mutual Assistance.

[67] League of Nations, *Arbitration, Security, and Reduction of Armaments,* 253.

and nearly all the vital questions affecting her national life were governed by the Treaties of Neuilly and Lausanne, that Bulgaria had consistently violated the military clauses of the former,[68] and that the latter imposed on Turkey no restrictions in regard to her military and naval forces. The conclusion was: "In order to provide for her security, Greece is therefore obliged to take military measures which she would have been glad to be able to reduce if she had been placed in more favorable circumstances."[69]

Siam referred to the "peculiarity" of her geographical situation and emphasized the fact that although military assistance was limited to the continent in which a conflict occurred, there was a chance that a colony of a European state might make an aggressive attack on an Asiatic country with forces drawn from Europe. To meet this situation the Siamese government suggested the possibility of a joint treaty of compulsory arbitration signed by Asiatic states together with European states having colonies in Asia.

Australia also found herself in a special situation in that "being a young country, Australia, in the adoption of measures for her own defence, has not yet attained the lowest point consistent with national safety; and therefore the obligation relating to reduction or limitation of armaments is without that special significance for us which it has for other and older States."[70] Moreover, the treaty would be an anomaly as far as Australia was concerned. That country, being an entire continent in itself, would derive neither obligations nor benefits with respect to military, naval, or air assistance.

The third group of criticisms of the draft Treaty of Mutual Assistance related to Article 4, which provided that "in the event of one or more of the High Contracting Parties becoming engaged in hostilities, the Council of the League of Nations shall decide, within four days of notification being addressed to the Secretary-General, which of the High Contracting Parties

---

[68] This drew an indignant disclaimer from Bulgaria.

[69] League of Nations, *Arbitration, Security, and Reduction of Armaments*, 259.

[70] Same, 234.

are the objects of aggression and whether they are entitled to claim the assistance provided under the Treaty."[71]

No fewer than twelve governments referred to the difficulty or impossibility of determining with accuracy, especially within the limited period of four days, the exceedingly important and delicate question of whether a state had committed "aggressive war" in the event of an outbreak of hostilities. France, in accepting the draft treaty, stated that although it was difficult to define all cases of aggression, it was possible to specify the most flagrant cases and that the phrase "within four days" might be changed to "as speedily as possible," allowing, for example, two weeks.

It is obvious that an acceptable definition of aggression and a reliable procedure for determining when an act of aggression has occurred are essential to a practicable system of collective security. Solution of the problem of effective applicability of a basic principle marks the dividing line between the purposive organization of consequences and the futile reiteration of desired but unattainable objectives. An international system in which disarmament is made to depend upon national security and national security in turn upon adverse differential treatment of any aggressor has as its indispensable condition the dependable expectation that a state which has become an aggressor will be named and proceeded against as such. If this cannot be accomplished, the entire system collapses.

Attempts to solve this difficulty are confronted with the dilemma that mutual assistance must be immediately available when needed, but it may not be possible at once to determine which state actually precipitated hostilities. The grave consequences of finding that a nation has committed aggression, the complexity of the issues involved in international controversies, the fact that no single test of aggression can be regarded as definitive in itself, the certainty that each party to a dispute would regard itself as acting in self-defense, the possibility that third states might disagree on the identity of

[71] League of Nations, *Reduction of Armaments*, 7.

the aggressor, the difficulty of arriving at the true facts of the situation, and the acknowledged influence of misleading propaganda are some of the considerations that plausibly suggest the unlikelihood of an immediate, accurate, and substantially unanimous decision. Yet delay and uncertainty will vitiate any conclusion which may be reached and will operate to the advantage of a state able to achieve a *fait accompli* by the sudden and unscrupulous use of force. And after all these difficulties have been overcome, there remains the problem of acting against a designated aggressor.

The Fifth Assembly, in 1924, gave a large share of its attention to the problems of disarmament and mutual security, specifically to the Protocol for the Pacific Settlement of International Disputes, more commonly referred to as the Geneva Protocol.[72]

The consideration which the Fifth Assembly and its committees devoted to disarmament and security was based upon the results of previous attempts to find a solution for the problems involved, taking as its point of departure the draft Treaty of Mutual Assistance and the comments of the various governments upon it. The principle of making the reduction of national armaments contingent upon the establishment of an international organization for the prevention of war was accepted and extended.

In substance, the objections to the draft Treaty of Mutual Assistance were met by the provision of a new scheme embodying the additional feature of compulsory pacific settlement of international disputes. Such a development had been suggested by a draft Treaty of Disarmament and Security drawn up by a group of American citizens and circulated among the members of the League in the summer of 1924.[73] This plan proposed that every dispute involving aggressive war, acts of

[72] See League of Nations, *Arbitration, Security, and Reduction of Armaments;* Walters, I, 268-76.

[73] Walters, I, 261-64; also see David Hunter Miller, *The Geneva Protocol,* 263-70; P. J. Noel-Baker, *The Geneva Protocol for the Pacific Settlement of International Disputes,* 18-19. Professor James T. Shotwell was the founder of the committee which prepared the "American Plan." See his *On the Rim of the Abyss,* 14-21.

aggression, or preparation for acts of aggression be submitted to the Permanent Court of International Justice; that the court have jurisdiction to decide, on the complaint of any signatory, whether or not in any given case such prohibited acts had been committed; and that any signatory which refused to accept the jurisdiction of the court be deemed an aggressor.

The work of the Fifth Assembly was based upon the formula, "arbitration,[74] security, disarmament." Disarmament had been made to depend upon the guarantee of security, and since the nonexecution of decisions reached by pacific methods would mean a reversion to the system of armed force, security in turn depended upon assurance that effective procedures for the pacific settlement of international controversies could be established. The fundamental principle of the Geneva Protocol was that national security was to be guaranteed and reduction of national armaments was to be attained by adverse differential treatment of any state which violated the provisions of an established procedure for the pacific settlement of international disputes.

Article 1 of the protocol provided that the signatory states would make every effort in their power to secure the introduction into the Covenant of amendments along the lines of the provisions of the protocol and that these provisions would be binding among themselves from the coming into force of the protocol. By Article 3 the signatory states would undertake to accept as compulsory *ipso facto* the jurisdiction of the Permanent Court of International Justice in the cases covered by paragraph 2 of Article 36 of the court. Provisions for compulsory pacific settlement of all international disputes were then elaborated.

This, in summary, was the plan offered to close the gaps of

[74] The word "arbitration" was used in connection with the Geneva Protocol to refer to the settlement of international disputes under the auspices of a machinery provided by the protocol and the Covenant of the League. The concept of arbitration differed from that of the Hague Conference in that in the Geneva Protocol arbitration was a part of the machinery for the compulsory pacific settlement of disputes, the principle of "equity" was applied, and acceptance of the result did not rest solely upon the good faith of the parties.

the Covenant, provide a pacific solution for all international disputes, guarantee national security against aggression, and bring about a reduction of national armaments. The Geneva Protocol would overcome the objections raised against the draft Treaty of Mutual Assistance by providing a dependable and universal guarantee. "The reduction of armaments will result, in the first place, from the general security created by a diminution of the dangers of war arising from the compulsory pacific settlement of all disputes. It will also ensue from the certainty which any State attacked will have of obtaining the economic and financial support of all the signatory States."[75]

The Geneva Protocol attempted to deal with the problems involved in the concept of "aggression" by providing an "adequate and automatic" test based on the principle of arbitration. Thus, "aggression" would be a resort to war in violation of the procedures of peaceful settlement laid down in the Covenant of the League and the Geneva Protocol; the protocol was designed to complement the Covenant, thereby insuring that every war would be prohibited and that any state which started a war would be penalized by international collective action.[76]

As soon as an aggressor was designated, the Council would call upon the signatory states to apply sanctions, in which case the obligations of Article 16 of the Covenant would immediately become operative. These obligations would require each of the signatory states "to co-operate loyally and effectively in support of the Covenant of the League of Nations, and in resistance to any act of aggression, in the degree to which its geographical position and its particular situation as regards armaments allow." In accepting the Geneva Protocol the sig-

[75] League of Nations, *Arbitration, Security, and Reduction of Armaments*, 361-62.

[76] The conclusion of the report of the Third Committee stated in part: "Our purpose was to make war impossible, to kill it, to annihilate it. To do this, we had to create a system for the pacific settlement of *all disputes* which might arise. Arbitration, therefore, is provided for every kind of dispute, and aggression is defined in such a way as to give no cause for hesitation when the Council has to take a decision. These reasons (that there should be no loopholes in the system) led us to fill in the gaps in the Covenant and to define the sanctions in such a way that there should be a sound and definite basis for the feeling of security" (same, 362-63).

natory states would further give a joint and several undertaking to come to the assistance of the nation attacked or threatened and to give each other mutual support.[77]

The Geneva Protocol was to go into effect as soon as it had been ratified by a majority of the permanent members of the Council and ten other members of the League, and a plan for the reduction of armaments as worked out by a disarmament conference had been accepted. In October, 1924, the Assembly passed a resolution recommending the adoption of the protocol. Fourteen states signed at the time, and several others followed their example a little later. However, in March, 1925, the British government presented to the Council of the League a statement rejecting the Geneva Protocol.[78] One argument advanced in support of this decision was that the method of "systematic completeness" had been rightly rejected by the framers of the Covenant, since "the objections to universal and compulsory arbitration might easily outweigh its theoretical advantages."[79]

The major objection of the British government, however, was that by the adoption of the protocol dangerous new responsibilities would devolve upon the members of the League. "Fresh classes of disputes are to be decided by the League; fresh possibilities of defying its decisions are thereby created; fresh occasions for the application of coercive measures follow as a matter of course."

It was pointed out that economic sanctions, which the Geneva Protocol had accepted as a weapon for restraining aggression, would operate in a way essentially different from that contemplated when the Covenant was adopted. Such measures, if simultaneously directed by all other states against a nation which was not economically self-sufficing, would be so powerful and effective that their use would seldom be neces-

[77] Same, 366. It was provided that in the contingency that both parties to a dispute were aggressors, sanctions would be applied to both of them.

[78] Great Britain, Foreign Office, *Statement by the Right Hon. Austen Chamberlain, M.P., on Behalf of His Majesty's Government, to the Council of the League of Nations, respecting the Protocol for the Pacific Settlement of International Disputes.*

[79] Same, 3.

sary. The situation would be entirely different, however, with the mere existence of powerful economic communities outside the League. The adoption of economic sanctions "might force trade into unaccustomed channels, but it could hardly stop it; and, though the offending States would no doubt suffer, there is no presumption that it would be crushed, or even that it would suffer most."[80]

Moreover, the protocol might actually operate in favor of an aggressor, since no preparations for war could be made from the moment when a dispute arose until proceedings for a pacific settlement had been concluded. This would permit an unscrupulous government to distribute its armed forces in the best possible strategic position and then start a dispute, whereupon the victim would be prohibited from strengthening its defensive position.[81]

In this connection the British communication referred to the "inherent impossibility of distinguishing, in any paper definition, military movements genuinely intended for defence, and only for defence, from movements with some ulterior aggressive purpose."[82]

The Geneva Protocol, in the view of the British government, would destroy the balance and alter the spirit of the Covenant. The emphasis laid upon sanctions and the elaboration of military procedure would, it was alleged, suggest the idea that the business of the League was not so much to promote "friendly co-operation and reasoned harmony" as to preserve peace by organizing war.[83]

The essence of the situation was that hesitation over disarmament was not prompted by fear of the gaps in the Covenant but by fear lest the Covenant would not be kept at all. "Brute force is what they [those who hesitate to disarm] fear,

[80] Same, 4. The point was also made that the danger of war might be increased by treating as aggressors nonmembers of the League who refused to accept the methods and decisions of the League.

[81] On the other hand, if the protocol were really effective, such a situation would be met by the combination of all other states against the aggressor.

[82] Great Britain, Foreign Office, 5.

[83] Such an emphasis on war was likened to the case of a man always brooding over the possibility of some severe surgical operation!

and only brute force enlisted in their defence can (as they believe) give them the security of which they feel the need."[84]

The British government in accordance with the above arguments took the position that the situation would not be bettered by the Geneva Protocol and suggested as an alternative that the Covenant be supplemented by "making special arrangements in order to meet special needs."[85]

The key to the attitude of the British government at this time lay in the judgment that acceptance of the Geneva Protocol would add "dangerous new responsibilities" upon the states which would have to take the lead in enforcing the system of collective security against an aggressor. Various practical considerations influenced this judgment. The fact alone that the United States was still absent from the League was sufficient to create a substantial difficulty for Great Britain if ever that country should be called upon to employ its fleet for an economic blockade in the application of sanctions. The opinion of the Dominion governments had been consulted, and it will be remembered that Canada was taking a leading part in trying to get the obligations of League membership decreased instead of increased. Great Britain, with its far-flung empire, its large navy, and its great economic and commercial interests, would perhaps carry the heaviest burden in the application of sanctions, and at the same time it would be exposed to opposition or at least reluctance on the part of its own dominions and also to possible serious difficulties in its relations with the United States. For these reasons alone the Geneva Protocol was not an agreement to be lightly accepted.

Then there were practical considerations with respect to the continent of Europe, particularly as concerned the Anglo-French-German triangle. France, with Germany in mind, wished to obtain additional guarantees of security as a prelude to reduction of armaments. Since the rejection of the League and of the tripartite guarantee by the United States, Great Britain had been unwilling to commit herself in any way to a unilateral underwriting of French security. In the immediate

[84] Great Britain, Foreign Office, 7.   [85] Same, 9.

postwar years British and French policy sharply diverged, notably in the disagreements over reparations and in French insistence on occupation of the Ruhr. It is true that by the time of the Fifth Assembly in 1924 this breach had been somewhat healed by the meeting of a reparations conference in London, the adoption of the Dawes Plan, and the evacuation of the Ruhr. The time for renewed collaboration seemed favorable, and an aspect of the guarantee proposals which constituted a grave defect from the British viewpoint had been adjusted. The draft Treaty of Mutual Assistance was based upon the concept "security before disarmament." The Geneva Protocol added the concept of arbitration. The significance of this lay in the fact that the system of collective security would not be available to a state which refused to submit its disagreements to third-party judgment. In the simplest terms, the draft Treaty of Mutual Assistance represented a French attempt to get help in enforcing the peace treaties; the Geneva Protocol represented a British attempt to force France to arbitrate her claims in return for additional guarantees of security.

Why, then, did Great Britain reject the Geneva Protocol? Rappard has pointed out[86] that, although the Labour and Conservative governments took opposing stands on the Geneva Protocol, the former rejected the draft Treaty of Mutual Assistance for practically the same reasons that the latter rejected the protocol. The answer, of course, lies in the fact that the Labour government considered "new responsibilities" dangerous without France's agreement to arbitrate her claims, while the Conservative government considered them dangerous even with that agreement. Without the support of Great Britain further consideration of the Geneva Protocol was pointless. Consequently the attempt to develop the League system in the direction of complete and universal guarantees was abandoned.

[86] *International Relations as Viewed from Geneva*, 182-84.

CHAPTER FOUR

Modified Application

THE PRINCIPLE of concern was accepted as a basis for international organization after World War I and then limited in the ways described in the preceding chapter. During 1925-1926 a new trend—toward modified application—was introduced. The limitation of general acceptance was replaced by an attempt to develop collective security on a more modest and gradual basis. The principle of concern was regionalized. The erection of a new system to replace the old was discarded for particular arrangements which, it was hoped, would develop in the direction of a more general or universal system.

It became clear that general acceptance of the principle of concern could not be implemented. Therefore, attention was turned to piecemeal or partial measures which had the double virtue of being consistent with the ideal of collective security and at the same time feasible under the circumstances. It was recalled that after all, politics is the art of the possible and that "leg over leg the dog went to Dover." If complete and universal acceptance of the principle of concern could not be effectively incorporated into international organization, the elaboration of more restricted measures might eventually arrive at the same goal. The attainment would be delayed, but there would be an immediate settlement of some of the danger spots to give the time required for fruition of the gradual evolutionary approach.

A series of settlements and agreements could supplement and integrate with each other, finally arriving at a system without gaps or loopholes. Since immediate realization of the goal was ruled out, a "step in the right direction" had everything to commend it. And enough steps in the right direction would lead to the goal, or at least much closer to it than futile insistence on immediate attainment. Up to 1925 the development of international organization through the League of Nations proceeded on the hypothesis that any war or threat of war was of concern to all the members. During 1925-1926 the viewpoint was adopted that some wars and threats are of more immediate concern than others, especially with respect to the members which would have to carry the chief burden of applying sanctions. The situations which were the most dangerous and of the greatest immediate concern logically called for prior attention. Collective security would be organized on a regional basis. This would be done in western Europe, then in other regions; and finally the various regional settlements could be integrated in a general system. Adoption of this concept and approach begins the period of modified application of the principle of concern.

1. LOCARNO

In rejecting the Geneva Protocol the British government had suggested as an alternative the procedure of supplementing the Covenant by special arrangements to meet special needs. This suggestion was accepted, and attention was turned to the matter of providing a guarantee against war in western Europe. The resulting agreements took the name of the town where they were signed—Locarno, in Switzerland.

The task of arriving at these agreements was essentially one of finding a formula that would meet French demands for additional security; that would serve as a basis for bringing Germany into the League of Nations; and that would offer Great Britain the means of participating in a regional contribution to collective security, as its government had proposed, but a contribution which would be severely restricted in its scope and not, in effect, a one-sided backing of France. Examination of the preliminary correspondence leading to the negotiation of the Locarno agreements reveals this clearly.

A German proposal for an agreement in Europe was made by Stresemann early in 1925 and communicated by the German ambassador in Paris to Herriot, President of the Council and French Minister of Foreign Affairs.[1] This suggestion was based on an undertaking by the powers interested in the Rhine, notably Great Britain, France, Italy, and Germany, to renounce war among themselves, with the United States as "trustee"; a comprehensive arbitration treaty; and acceptance by Germany of the territorial *status quo* in the Rhineland, as well as guarantees of the demilitarization of that area as provided in Articles 42 and 43 of the Treaty of Versailles.

France and Great Britain corresponded in order to arrive at a mutually agreeable reply to the German memorandum. A draft proposal incorporating the position of France was forwarded to the British government in a note of May 12. The reply suggested in this document would accept the German proposal as "an earnest of pacific intentions" but raised certain questions on which agreement would be necessary as a preliminary step for further negotiations. The main points outlined by France were: Germany must enter the League of Nations, with the same obligations and rights as other members; no revision in the peace treaties could be considered; Belgium must be included in the proposed Rhineland pact, and such an agreement could not affect existing provisions for the occupation of the Rhineland; arbitration treaties should apply to any disputes whatever and should leave room for coercive action only in case of failure to observe the agreements to be concluded. The question of eastern Europe was raised rather obliquely by reference to the necessity of similar agreements of those neighbors of Germany "who, without being parties to the suggested Rhineland Pact, are signatories of the Treaty of Versailles." Finally, the French government suggested the

---

[1] George Glasgow, *From Dawes to Locarno;* Walters, *A History of the League of Nations,* I, 285-94.

whole series of agreements be co-ordinated in a general convention to be placed under the auspices of the League of Nations.

A British request of May 19 for explanation and clarification of certain points in the French draft was answered on May 25. Then on May 28 Chamberlain stated in a memorandum the conditions on which Great Britain could concur in the proposed reply to the German proposal. Any new obligation which the British government undertook must be specific and limited to the existing territorial arrangement on the western frontier of Germany. The French draft went considerably beyond what the British government could endorse consistently with this principle; an example was the broad scope of the proposed arbitration agreements, which Great Britain would not be prepared to underwrite as one co-ordinated and indivisible system, although the various agreements might well come into force simultaneously. Parenthetically it may be remarked that the great care which the British government took to intimate that it would enter into only severely restricted agreements was reflected not only in the statement of its general position, but also in the use of such language as "subject to a careful examination of the actual terms ultimately proposed," "proposals whose exact shape could only be determined when the time was reached for considering a draft instrument," and "must reserve its liberty to define more precisely at the proper time the interpretation to be placed upon them."

The British memorandum offered a substitute draft reply in which it would be prepared to concur. This draft was framed in such a way as to place strict limitations wherever the French draft had stated or implied a broad guarantee. One example of this was in references to arbitration treaties. The French draft, as has been noted, contemplated a general system of such treaties to be guaranteed along with the Rhineland pact. The British substitute draft limited this to an arbitration treaty between France and Germany. Where the French draft said that there should be no room for coercive action "save in case of failure to observe the provisions of the various treaties and agreements contemplated in the present note," the British substitute was "save where such action may be taken consistently with the provisions of treaties in force between the parties." Then, after limiting the scope of any arbitration treaty supplementary to the proposed Rhineland pact, the British substitute draft qualified the statement that observance would be assured by a joint and several guarantee by adding: "so as to ensure that any failure to refer a dispute to arbitration or to carry out an award would, if coupled with a resort to hostilities, bring the guarantee into immediate operation. In the absence of a resort to hostilities, the Council of the League shall propose what steps should be taken to give effect to the treaty."

Another example of the difference between the British and French approaches at the time was the omission by the former of a paragraph in the French draft which in effect called for a system of arbitration treaties with Germany's eastern neighbors. In the same connection, where the French draft had tied up the proposed Rhineland pact with the "peace of Europe," the British substitute changed the language to make such a pact an "essential step" toward the peace of Europe.

The crux of the difference between the French and British governments was the question of whether the guarantees would be restricted to western Europe only or extended to the eastern boundaries of Germany as well. Great Britain was willing to participate only in the former. France considered the latter also essential. The French viewpoint was expressed in a note of June 4 replying to the British suggestions for a substitute draft. In the French opinion any attempt to modify by force the state of affairs created by the peace treaties would constitute a menace to peace to which France could not remain indifferent. An essential condition of the proposed Rhineland pact was that France would retain its liberty of action to go to the assistance of states parties to the Treaty of Versailles but not directly interested in the Rhineland. Therefore the French government proposed to reinsert the paragraph omitted in the British substitute draft, but changed to give signatories of the proposed Rhineland pact the option of constituting themselves the guarantors of arbitration treaties between Germany and her eastern neighbors. Thus France, unable to persuade Great Britain to participate in such a guarantee, insisted on the liberty of making it an essential element in her own policy. In this Great Britain concurred, and a sufficient identity of French and British views was reached to permit a reply under date of June 16 to the German proposal of the preceding February.

The Franco-British discussions over broad versus limited commitments toward guarantees of security turned to the Franco-German discussions over broad versus limited conditions for the acceptance of the German proposal. The German government wanted to restrict the proposed agreement to the territorial *status quo* on its western boundary. The French government desired a reaffirmation of the entire Versailles system, including an acceptance by Germany of the territorial *status quo* in the east and of all existing treaty provisions for the Rhineland. A compromise basis for negotiation had to be reached, just as it had been necessary between France and Great Britain.

The German government counterreplied in a note of July 20. Three major points were raised. The first showed the German anxiety not to preclude questions of revising the peace treaties. The relevant part of the statement was:

The conclusion of a Pact of Security as outlined in the German suggestions does not represent a modification of existing treaties. There should, therefore, be no need for special statements in this respect. The German Government consider as self-evident that it is not meant to exclude for all future time the possibility of adapting existing treaties at the proper time to changed circumstances by way of peaceful agreement. They may point out that even the Covenant of the League of Nations allows for such necessities.

If the Allied Governments emphasize, for instance, that the Pact of Security must not affect the treaty provisions in force concerning the military occupation of German territories, it is correct that the German Memorandum has not made the conclusion of the Pact dependent on a modification of those provisions. But should the Allied Governments intend to set those provisions up as a sacrosanct for the future, the German Government would, in answer to this, like to point out that the conclusion of a Security Pact would represent an innovation of such importance that it could not but react on the conditions in the occupied territories and the questions of occupation in general.[2]

The second point raised by the German government was its apprehension about a possible unilateral determination to apply coercive measures for an alleged violation of one of the treaties or agreements. The third point had to do with the conditions of admission to the League of Nations. Germany was still insisting on some recognition of her special status as a disarmed power and the danger of involvement in the armed conflict of third countries. Germany, as a member of the League, could "only be considered as enjoying equal rights when her disarmament is followed by the general disarmament provided for by the Covenant of the League of Nations and the preamble to Part V of the Treaty of Versailles. Therefore, if the immediate entrance of Germany into the League of Nations is to be rendered possible, a solution has to be found to tide over the time till general disarmament has become a reality. The solution would have to pay due regard to the special military and economical as well as to the special geographical situation of Germany."[3]

The French reply, on August 24, to these German observations again precluded any question of modifying any of the provisions of the peace treaties in connection with the proposed agreements, saying, "However liberal the spirit, however pacific the intentions, with which France is ready to pursue the present negotiations, she cannot surrender her rights." The German contention about recognition of her special position in relation to the League was again rejected. It was stated in part:

The Allies are convinced that membership of the League of Nations would provide Germany, once she has entered the League, with the most efficacious method of establishing her requirements as other States have done in regard to their own interests. The entry of Germany into the League of Nations is the only solid basis for a mutual guarantee and a European agreement. It is not, in fact, from outside that a State can properly express reservations, which

2 Glasgow, 160.   3 Same, 162.

would thus assure the character of conditions; it is from within that it can submit its wishes to the Council in the exercise of a right common to all the States members of the League.[4]

Finally, the French note of August 24 rejected the German apprehensions about the interpretation of arbitral agreements as ill founded but in turn expressed the fear that German reservations would restrict such agreements to the point that they would not be effective in the maintenance of peace.

It was then agreed that a further exchange of preliminary views would serve no useful purpose, and the actual negotiation of the Locarno agreements proceeded. Accordingly, representatives of the German, Belgian, British, French, Italian, Polish, and Czechoslovak governments met at Locarno from October 5 to 16, 1925, in order to arrive at some agreement on the problem of European security.

As a result there were concluded[5] a Treaty of Mutual Guarantee between Germany, Belgium, France, Great Britain, and Italy; an arbitration convention between Germany and France; and an arbitration treaty between Germany and Poland, and an identical treaty between Poland and Czechoslovakia. A collective note was sent to Germany on the interpretation of Article 16.[6] And finally, France signed treaties with Poland and Czechoslovakia providing for reciprocal supplementary guarantees.

The basic provision of the Locarno agreements was a collective and several guarantee of the boundaries between Germany and France, and between Germany and Belgium, by these three countries together with Great Britain and Italy. Germany and France, and Germany and Belgium, agreed that they would not attack, invade, or resort to war against each other except in the exercise of the right of legitimate defense;[7]

---

[4] Same, 164.   [5] League of Nations, *Treaty Series*, 44:289-363.

[6] See Chapter III, section 2.

[7] "Legitimate defense" was defined as resistance to a violation of the undertaking against attack or resort to war or to "a flagrant breach of Articles 42 and 43 of the . . . Treaty of Versailles, if such breach constitutes an unprovoked act of aggression and by reason of the assembly of armed forces in the demilitarised zone, immediate action is necessary" (Article 2).

action under Article 16 of the Covenant; or action as a result of a decision made in pursuance of Article 15, paragraph 7, of the Covenant, provided that the action was directed against the state which was the first to attack. In view of these agreements Germany and Belgium, and Germany and France, undertook to settle by peaceful means all questions of every kind which might arise between them.

An alleged violation of the undertaking not to attack or resort to war, or of Articles 42 and 43 of the Treaty of Versailles, would be brought to the attention of the Council of the League, and upon its finding that such a violation had been committed, the signatories of the treaty would immediately come to the assistance of the state against which the violation was directed. In case of a *flagrant* breach of the same undertakings, each of the other contracting parties would be bound to come to the assistance of the victim as soon as they had satisfied themselves that an unprovoked act of aggression had been committed and immediate action had become necessary. Nevertheless, the Council would be apprised of the question, and the signatories would be bound to follow its recommendations if concurred in by all the members other than the parties to the dispute. Also, the recommendations of the Council were to be followed in case a signatory, without committing the mentioned violations, should refuse to submit a dispute to peaceful settlement or to comply with an arbitral award or judicial decision.

The Locarno arbitration agreements provided that all disputes in which the parties were in conflict over their respective rights and which could not be settled amicably by the normal methods of diplomacy would be submitted to an arbitral tribunal or to the Permanent Court of International Justice. By agreement, prior resort could be had to the machinery of a permanent conciliation commission, established by each of the Locarno arbitration agreements. All disputes which were not otherwise settled amicably and which could not be solved by a judicial decision were to be referred to the processes of conciliation. If agreement could not be reached in this way, the question might, at the request of either party, be brought before the Council of the League to be dealt with according to Article 15 of the Covenant.

Such, in summary, was the series of agreements and guarantees reached at Locarno during October, 1925. Their effective date was dependent upon German entry into the League of Nations. This was accomplished the next year, and the Locarno agreements went into force on September 14, 1926.[8] With reference to the achievement, the final protocol of the conference stated: "The representatives of the Governments represented here declare their firm conviction that the entry into force of these treaties and conventions will contribute greatly in bringing about a moral relaxation of the tension between nations, that it will help powerfully towards the solution of many political or economic problems in accordance with the interests and sentiments of peoples, and that, in strengthening peace and security in Europe, it will hasten on effectively the disarmament provided for in Article 8 of the Covenant of the League of Nations."[9]

The Locarno agreements went a considerable way toward meeting the aspirations of the three Great Powers most directly concerned, as put forth in their preliminary correspondence. France received a guarantee of her Rhineland boundary backed up by Great Britain and Italy, a sort of reinsurance treaty with two of her eastern allies, and saw Germany undertake the obligations of League membership. Germany for her part was admitted to the League on an equality with other members and received an interpretation of her obligations toward the application of sanctions which in effect left such a decision in her own hands. Great Britain was able to participate in a regional arrangement as a contribution to collective security, but an arrangement which was confined to an area considered essential for British national defense anyhow. An alternative for the Geneva Protocol was found without any real extension of British commitments, since in any event she could not stand idly by if France or Belgium were attacked.

What was the effect of the Locarno agreements on the

[8] League of Nations, *Treaty Series*, 44:291.   [9] Same, 299.

League of Nations? They were placed within the framework of the League, as the French had insisted all along. The Council of the League was given important responsibilities in connection with disputes or violations by the arbitration agreements as well as by the Treaty of Mutual Guarantee itself. Also, it was provided by Article 7 of the latter that "The present Treaty, which is designed to ensure the maintenance of peace, and is in conformity with the Covenant of the League of Nations, shall not be interpreted as restricting the duty of the League to take whatever action may be deemed wise and effectual to safeguard the peace of the world."[10]

On the other hand, the Locarno agreements could be interpreted as paying formal respect to the League but recognizing that no real dependence was being placed in its efficacy. The provision for terminating the Locarno agreements read like a confession of weakness on the part of the League. Article 8 of the main treaty, immediately after the statement just quoted, provided for its registration with the League and then continued: "It shall remain in force until the Council, acting on a request of one or other of the High Contracting Parties notified to the other signatory Powers three months in advance, and voting at least by a two-thirds' majority, decides that the League of Nations ensures sufficient protection to the High Contracting Parties; the Treaty shall cease to have effect on the expiration of a period of one year from such decision."[11]

Only time would tell whether the Locarno agreements would be the starting point of a stronger League or of a system of alliances only nominally consistent with the principles and objectives of that organization. The outlook in 1926 seemed to have been overwhelmingly hopeful. "Locarno ended the war" was a widely accepted judgment.[12] Victors and vanquished were becoming equal collaborators, and definite progress was being made in settling some of the major difficulties in Europe. Chamberlain said, "These treaties are the real dividing line between the war years and those of peace"; and

[10] Same, 295.   [11] Same.
[12] See Harold Quigley, *From Versailles to Locarno.*

Briand, "We are now only Europeans." The effective re-establishment of peace was to take place through the "spirit of Locarno." The Locarno agreements portended real progress in disarmament, thus beginning "the dimilitarization of human society, a reversal of the insidious and devastating perversion of life and riches to military ends which the last two generations of European statesmen thrust upon the peoples of the world."[13]

A British writer, George Glasgow, offered a typical example of the more optimistic opinions of the time:

So far as the diplomatic opinion of the seven countries is concerned, the only important thing done at Locarno—but it is all important—is that those countries have openly committed themselves to a pacifist policy in the future. For the first time in diplomatic history Great Powers have surrendered their historic "right to make war" . . . and it will be next to impossible for them to recapture, even if they wanted to recapture, so dangerous a "right". The value of Locarno may be put in this way. Hitherto the mass of sensible people have longed for peace, but fear and stupid tradition have made them disbelieve in it, and the whole conception of international relations has been based on the hypothesis that there would be war, somewhere at some time. The difference now is that, whereas national honour in the past was bound up with war, it is now bound up with peace. After Locarno war is synonymous with national dishonour. The plunge has been taken in favour of pacifism, for the first time in European history.[14]

The same author also quoted a conversation with Edward Benes of Czechoslovakia, in which the latter said in part: "For the first time since the war the four Great Powers say the same thing. It is a tremendous advance on anything that has yet been accomplished. In one sense it is a partial Protocol, for whereas the Protocol aimed at the universal outlawry of war, the Pact outlaws it so far as one particular danger spot is concerned. For the first time in diplomatic history nations have renounced their sovereign 'right to make war.' That fact brings with it an entirely new conception of international war and peace."[15]

---

[13] P. J. Noel-Baker, *Disarmament*, 3.　　[14] *From Dawes to Locarno*, 123.
[15] Same, 126.

However, in a foreword to the same book former prime minister Ramsay MacDonald, whose government had endorsed the Geneva Protocol, saw in the Locarno agreements an opportunity rather than a significant achievement. One of his comments is of particular interest. He said:

Locarno does not face any of the problems that could be, in the widest stretch of imagination, an immediate cause of a European war. I have never met anybody yet . . . who sits in a European Foreign Office and who believes that in our lifetime, or in anybody's lifetime, there is going to be a war between France and Germany directly and specifically caused over the Rhine frontier. That is not how the war will come in Europe. If anybody thinks that by getting agreement on the Rhine frontier we have made European war impossible, he should think again. If there should be another European war, it is perfectly true that the Rhine frontier will be an element in it, but it will be raised only after war has broken out.[16]

Another British writer published a book[17] containing a chapter entitled "Back to Common Sense *via* Locarno." The argument for this judgment was based on the comparison between general and regional pacts, to the great disadvantage of the former. This matter is so important to the principle of concern in international organization that a rather lengthy quotation seems appropriate:

It is nevertheless true to say that there is between the *régime* of the League and the *régime* of bi-partite agreements or regional pacts a real and fundamental difference of principle, at all events in regard to the motive for which the stipulated assistance is afforded. The opposition is still more apparent between the more highly developed system of the Protocol and the system of such limited agreements or pacts. The one system seeks security by means of international guarantees and sanctions; the community of nations imposes peace by bringing its combined force to bear upon the law-breaker. In the other system security is based on self-help. It is the solidarity of interests of the nations concerned

[16] Same, ix.
[17] J. M. Spaight, *Pseudo-Security*. By this term he meant "the kind of security which the League of Nations purports to afford to its members by preventing *by combined force* either certain wars, as under the existing system, or all wars, as under the developed system proposed in the Geneva Protocol of 1924" (p. 1).

which binds them together in a regional pact; it is a wider and more unselfish motive which inspires the general scheme.

Self-help is none the less self-help when it takes the form of assistance rendered to an ally. You help your ally or he helps you because you or he would suffer if either were attacked in isolation and defeated. It is immediate self-interest which is the motive for the rendering of aid. Quite different is the basic impulse in the league of peace. There the underlying motive is a wider one, a nobler one, perhaps, than that which inspires the regional pact or alliance. It is not, of course, pure knight-errantry. It embraces the selfish motive, too, for the individual shares with the community in the blessings of unbroken peace. But the member of a league of peace must look above and beyond the end of his own self-preservation to another end which will bring to him, it is to be supposed, his reward in the satisfaction of saving not only his skin but his soul alive. Something over and above patriotism must be the compelling influence. A league of peace that is not inspired by an abundant international charity—as well as by a very plentiful measure of faith and hope, which will assuredly be needed—is nothing.[18]

The great and abiding merit of regional pacts is that they do not confront one with the inescapable dilemma presented by any and every system of international guarantees and sanctions such as that represented by the Protocol of 1924: that if security is to be safeguarded the system will be unacceptable to some nations because the commitments are too onerous and rigid, and if the commitments are loose and discretionary it will be unacceptable to others because it does not give security. Security and commitments go hand in hand in regional pacts. The security which is afforded is geographically limited but within its limits it is reasonably strong, because the motive for the rendering of the stipulated assistance is the practical and compelling one of *self-interest*.[19]

Thus, the regionalization of the principle of concern posed the question of whether that fact would be a step in its general implementation or in effect the abandonment of that principle for a reliance solely upon a self-help for such control of international conflict as it might be possible to organize.

---

[18] Same, 132-33.   [19] Same, 145-46.

2. Improving the Means of Preventing War

The period of modified application of the principle of concern happened to coincide with a renewed attack on the problem of disarmament. It will be remembered that the Geneva Protocol had developed from attempts to solve this very question. After the conclusion of the Locarno agreements there was a double reason for intensifying the search for a solution. First, the obligation of the Covenant remained, and with German entry into the League the promise of general, rather than unilateral, disarmament could not be ignored. In the second place, the very success of the Locarno agreements and the optimism accompanying them offered a basis for hopes of substantial success. These reasons were, of course, in addition to the continuing realization of the burdens and dangers of a high level of national armaments.

The connection made by the League at this time between disarmament and international organization for the control of conflict may be expressed in the words of a resolution adopted by the Assembly on September 26, 1927. Speaking of assuring the success of the work of disarmament, the Assembly expressed its conviction "that the principal condition of this success is that every State should be sure of not having to provide unaided for its security by means of its own armaments and should be able to rely also on the organised collective action of the League of Nations."[20]

Accordingly, consideration of the means for preventing war was carried on in close connection with the work of preparing for the Disarmament Conference (which was finally convened at Geneva in 1932).

Three agreements on the place of war in international organization may be noted here.[21] The first of these was the Assembly

[20] League of Nations, *Records of the Eighth Ordinary Session of the Assembly*, Plenary Meetings, 177.

[21] There were also various proposals and studies designed to expedite the application of sanctions, should the occasion arise. Examples were arrangements to expedite communications with Geneva in the event of an emergency

resolution of September 24, 1927, condemning wars of aggression and declaring that pacific means must be employed to settle disputes which arise among nations.[22] This resolution had been presented on September 9 by the representative of Poland, who urged its adoption as "a great world declaration of confidence." The Geneva Protocol had been rejected, and no complete system for the prevention of war was immediately feasible. But, he continued, "Just as some public demonstration of the wish for mutual understanding often precedes the conclusion of an alliance between two States, so the solemn renunciation of all acts of aggression would constitute a solid foundation for the great mechanism of guarantees and security."[23] The Italian delegate opposed the resolution on the ground that it was superfluous, futile, and tended to discredit the League and undermine its prestige by putting it in a position by which its recommendations were certain to be disregarded by governments. The proposal was later referred to the Third Committee (on Reduction of Armaments), which approved it by acclamation after a brief discussion. There was no debate on it at the time of its adoption by the Assembly itself.

One might hesitate to call the Assembly resolution against aggression a "mere gesture." However, it was certainly confined to an expression of opinion, without legal force and without any suggestion of binding the members of the League in any way. This was expressly stated at the time of its adoption by the delegate who made the proposal. It was presented for its "moral and educative effect."

The second measure arising out of considerations associated with preparations for a disarmament conference was the General Act for the Pacific Settlement of International Disputes, endorsed by the Assembly in a resolution of September 26,

and the Finnish proposal for financial assistance to victims of aggression. Such proposals were matters of procedure and method, and did not have any direct implications for defining the status of international conflict under international organization.

[22] League of Nations, *Records of the Eighth Assembly*, 155.

[23] Same, Plenary Meetings, 83.

1928. A Preparatory Commission for the Disarmament Conference had been set up by the Council in December, 1925,[24] and given the task suggested by its name. At its meeting on November 30, 1927, the Preparatory Commission constituted a Committee on Arbitration and Security to consider measures for giving all states the guarantees necessary to enable them to fix the level of their armaments at the lowest possible figure.[25] This committee in its studies and discussions basically took the approach of attempting to extend the idea of regional security pacts and to expand the coverage of procedures for pacific settlement. The logic of Locarno was not lost. Efforts to develop a complete system of collective security were to be superseded by more modest arrangements, with the twin virtues of current acceptability and promise of eventual universality. In the words of the committee's report of February, 1928:

> This method of special or collective treaties appears at the present moment to be the only practical means which can be recommended to States in search of more effective guarantees of security.
>
> Those nations which consider that the general measure of security afforded by the Covenant is inadequate for their needs, and which, more particularly in view of their geographical situation, feel themselves more liable than others to be drawn into a war in case of a failure of all the machinery designed to prevent armed conflicts, must at the present moment regard the conclusion of security pacts with other States in the same geographical area as the only practical or possible form of supplementary guarantee. Even if the other Members of the League of Nations cannot give their effective guarantee to such treaties they can at least accord them their moral support and do everything in their power to facilitate their conclusion, provided always that such treaties are conceived in the spirit of the Covenant of the League and are co-ordinated within its provisions.[26]

In this way, the "network of preventive measures" would be extended.

The committee's study of arbitration procedures was based upon a "Memorandum on Arbitration and Security" submitted

---

[24] League of Nations, *Official Journal*, 1926, pp. 164-69.
[25] Same, 1928, p. 610.   [26] Same, 653. Paragraph numbering omitted.

by the representative of Finland.[27] His analysis of the procedure already being followed revealed three general types of
conventions in force. The first, represented by thirty treaties
registered with the League, called for the submission of all
disputes to arbitration. The second, represented by the Locarno agreements, provided for the arbitration of juridical
disputes and conciliation of the others. The third type, used
chiefly by Switzerland and the Scandinavian states, provided
for conciliation only. Various reservations were found to apply
to all three types of conventions. It was recommended that
procedures for pacific settlement be developed by extension of
coverage and by co-ordination.

At the same time, a "Memorandum on Security Questions"
was submitted by the Greek delegate.[28] The basic approach
of this study is shown by the first three paragraphs of its conclusions:

> It is impossible at present to contemplate the conclusion of a
> general agreement—adding to the obligations assumed under the
> Covenant—with a view to giving the nations greater security.
> States which require wider guarantees of security should seek
> them in the form of separate or collective agreements for non-
> aggression, arbitration and mutual assistance, or simply for non-
> aggression.
> Regional pacts comprising non-aggression, arbitration and mutual
> assistance represent the completest form of security agreement, and
> the one which can most easily be brought into harmony with the
> system of the Covenant. Such pacts should always include the fol-
> lowing provisions:
>   (a) A prohibition to resort to force;
>   (b) The organisation of pacific procedures for the settlement of
> all disputes;
>   (c) The establishment of a system of mutual assistance, to oper-
> ate in conjunction with the duties of the League Council.[29]

Accepting these conclusions, the Committee on Arbitration
and Security undertook the preparation of a series of model

[27] Same, 654-60.
[28] Same, 660-70. A third study was the Rutgers "Memorandum on Articles
10, 11, and 16 of the Covenant."
[29] Same, 669. Paragraph numbering omitted.

conventions to expedite the expansion and co-ordination of procedures for arbitration and security. All a state had to do was
to pick out the provisions to which it was willing to commit
itself and sign on the dotted line. As other nations did likewise,
an integrated system of pacific procedures would automatically
be extended over wider and wider areas.

The General Act for the Pacific Settlement of International
Disputes[30] contained four chapters. The first included a general conciliation convention, which merely codified and reproduced the provisions of a large number of bilateral conciliation
treaties already in force. It had the merit of providing one
multilateral agreement, making the negotiation of individual
bilateral conventions no longer necessary. The second chapter
of the General Act added compulsory arbitration for all justiciable disputes, which would be referred to the Permanent Court
of International Justice or to an arbitral tribunal by agreement
of the parties. For nonjusticiable disputes a procedure of compulsory conciliation was provided. If this failed, disputes
would be referred to the Council of the League for handling
under Article 15 of the Covenant. The third chapter provided
the most comprehensive procedure of all. It extended judicial
settlement and arbitration to all disputes without distinction.
Justiciable disputes would go to the Permanent Court and
others to a special arbitral tribunal.

The final chapter contained the general provisions relating
to the entire document. The act allowed partial accessions.
That is, a state could accede to all four chapters at once or to
the separate chapters, with a choice of three methods of combining them. The act could be accepted by a nation with or
without stipulated reservations. Further elasticity was obtained
by allowing an acceding state to extend the scope of its undertakings at any time by a simple declaration. Thus, by an in-
genious scheme every shade of choice from the mildest kind
of conciliation to the most comprehensive acceptance of com-

---

[30] League of Nations, *Treaty Series*, 93:343-63. For reports and discussions
on the General Act and the accompanying draft agreements, see *Official
Journal*, 1928, pp. 610-706; *Records of the Ninth Ordinary Session of the Assembly*, Plenary Meetings, 167-84, 217-21, 486-527.

pulsory arbitration was made available to any country by the mere act of accession. It would come into effect when accepted by any two nations and would remain open for accession indefinitely.

The General Act found a considerable measure of acceptance, as more than twenty governments acceded to some or all its provisions.[31]

In addition to the General Act the Committee on Arbitration and Security drew up three model bilateral conventions, the provisions of which corresponded to the terms of the first three chapters, respectively, of the General Act. Thus, the flexibility of the entire scheme extended even to a choice between the bilateral and multilateral approaches. The recommendations of procedures for pacific settlement were completed by three draft resolutions. One recommended the General Act and the model bilateral conventions; the second was designed to facilitate wider acceptance of the Optional Clause of the Permanent Court; and the last was concerned with the good offices of the Council in connection with the negotiation of procedures of pacific settlement.

With respect to security questions model draft treaties were offered for consideration. The first, a model collective treaty, was the most comprehensive. It included three features taken from the Locarno agreements—nonaggression, pacific settlement, and mutual assistance. However, it differed from the Locarno pact in that it contained no special territorial guarantees, no guarantees by third states, no special provision for cases of flagrant aggression, and no stipulations regarding demilitarized zones. The second model security treaty was similar to the first, except that it omitted the feature of mutual assistance. The third model treaty had the same provisions as the second, but was bilateral in form. These three draft models also carried with them appropriate resolutions.

Only brief mention need be made of the General Convention to Improve the Means of Preventing War. Its basic idea was that in the event of a dispute between them being brought

---

[31] Manley O. Hudson, *International Legislation*, IV, 2529.

before the Council of the League, the signatory states would observe certain conservatory measures recommended by the Council to prevent an aggravation of the situation. Such measures would include, for example, the evacuation of certain zones or the fixing of lines not to be passed by military forces. This draft convention was approved by the Assembly[32] on September 26, 1931, with the hope that a large number of governments would ratify it prior to the scheduled opening of the Disarmament Conference on February 2, 1932. Unfortunately, the Manchurian incident had started only a few days before the adoption of the convention by the Assembly, and the situation did not prove conducive to the acceptance of its obligations by the member states. Sufficient ratifications were never obtained to bring it into force.

The attempt during the period 1926-1932 to facilitate preparations for a disarmament conference by working out procedures for pacific settlement and guarantees of security returned to a technique used prior to World War I. The Hague Conventions and other agreements such as the Bryan conciliation treaties had been based upon the idea of reducing the likelihood of war by providing alternative methods of settlement and cooling-off periods. The General Act of 1928 and its companion efforts were likewise based upon reducing the likelihood of war by the provision of alternative procedures and by promises of self-restraint in the use of aggressive force.[33] Before World War I the failure of the pacific alternatives and a resort to war brought no penalties against an aggressor *per se*. Neutrality was incumbent upon third states, unless their in-

[32] League of Nations, *Official Journal*, 1931, pp. 1123-24, 1452-60, 2305-307; *Records of the Twelfth Ordinary Session of the Assembly*, Plenary Meetings, 147-49, 237-43. This draft convention was worked out by a special committee of the Council and the Third Committee of the Assembly. It may be of interest to note that the Japanese delegate on the special committee refrained from voting on the proposal during a meeting in May, 1931. See John W. Wheeler-Bennett, *Disarmament and Security since Locarno, 1925-1931*, 300-306.

[33] There was also some revival of the idea of limiting the severity of war, as in pre-War conventions. There was much discussion of restricting submarine warfare and other measures considered unjustifiably inhumane. A protocol for the prohibition of the use in war of asphyxiating, poisonous, or other gases, and of bacteriological warfare, was signed in 1925 and was ratified by a number of states.

terests or circumstances brought them into the war as participant belligerents. On the other hand, violation of supplementary obligations of pacific settlement after World War I would leave the Covenant of the League applicable in situations covered by its terms. The General Act was integrated with the Covenant, but it did not pretend to enlarge the scope of the latter. Violation of an undertaking under the General Act presumably would not make a state subject to sanctions unless the Covenant were also violated.

Under the older system there was an interest in reducing the likelihood of war but no collective penalty for a breach of the peace. Under the newer system the interest in reducing the likelihood of war was accompanied by provisions for adverse differential treatment of a state resorting to war in some, but not all, cases. Modified application of the principle of concern represented a limited and partial reliance upon it in international organization. Techniques of arbitration and conciliation were applicable under both systems because their successful use in contributing to the maintenance of peace would assist in the establishment of collective security. The Hague Conventions and similar agreements were procedural restrictions upon the resort to war. The General Act of 1928 attempted to use the same type of procedural restrictions to fill the gaps in the Covenant. If alternative procedures could confine the free sweep of the unfettered right to wage war before 1914, they could be adapted to whittle down the wars remaining licit in 1928.

One cannot escape the conclusion that the General Act, with the related measures described above, was a slight contribution indeed to that security upon which disarmament depended. But although the contributions were slight and insufficient, it is difficult to see how any others were possible of accomplishment in the circumstances. The dilemma of disarmament was that adequate measures to achieve security were not feasible (because they would not be accepted), and feasible measures were not adequate. The former Allies would not disarm until they felt more secure. The Covenant of the League, after the process of limitation, did not give them the requisite feeling of security. The Geneva Protocol, intended to enhance security, was not accepted. Locarno did provide some increase in security, but it was not felt to be enough. If, then, the Covenant plus Locarno did not give enough security and arrangements analogous to the Geneva Protocol could not be put into effect, what path to peace was open? About the only practicable course was the one adopted. The attempt was made to find something stronger than the Covenant plus Locarno, but not strong enough to suffer the fate of the protocol. The result was moderately acceptable but entirely inadequate.

3. THE PACT OF PARIS

Signature of the Pact of Paris—or Treaty for the Renunciation of War—on August 27, 1928, was an important event in the process of redefining the position of war in international law and organization. By its provisions practically every state in the world obtained a right or vested interest in the maintenance of peace. Resort to war could not be considered a matter of legal indifference. Furthermore, the United States for the first time accepted an international obligation based upon the principle of concern. The pact did not mark the abandonment of a policy of neutrality by the United States government, but it did provide an optional basis for discrimination between participants in a war and it did involve the acceptance of a principle whose implications were incompatible with an unqualified dependence upon the concepts of traditional neutrality. The Pact of Paris, of course, became a "dead letter" in the cycle of events leading to the second World War, but it turned out to have an enduring significance when it was used as a basis for indictment of the principal German and Japanese "war criminals." The theory in this connection was that the legal right of a state to resort to war (aggression) had been removed by ratification of the Pact of Paris and that the initiation of war was the act of an illegal conspiracy for which the government officials involved were individually and personally responsible.

The idea of a solemn and universal condemnation and renunciation of war was initiated during negotiations for a treaty of perpetual friendship between France and the United States, and was developed into a multilateral agreement with almost universal acceptance. The pact, in the form finally agreed upon, stated that the contracting parties "condemn recourse to war for the solution of international controversies, and renounce it as an instrument of national policy in their relations with one another" and "agree that the settlement or solution of all disputes or conflicts of whatever nature or of whatever origin they may be, which may arise among them, shall never be sought except by pacific means."[34]

To what extent did the Pact of Paris modify the acceptance of the principle of concern in international law and organization? In the interpretation of the pact, both practical and theoretical, the fundamental question involved its relevance to the principle of adverse differential treatment of a nation which resorted to war. In other words, in what position would a violator of the pact stand with respect to third states?

First of all, the Pact of Paris was important as a solemn declaration of governmental policies and a considered reflection of public opinion in nearly all states of the world. By it war was publicly and officially repudiated and renounced. Nations covenanted with one another to remove war as a legitimate method of settling any disputes whatsoever which might arise among them.

But the Pact of Paris was more than a statement of policy, which might be changed at any time. As a treaty it was an instrument of international law, with legal consequences flowing from it just as from any treaty. The questions of the rights or obligations of a state under the pact in any specific case would be a matter of treaty interpretation, for which it would

[34] For the negotiation and conclusion of the pact, see David Hunter Miller, *The Peace Pact of Paris;* Denys P. Myers, *Origin and Conclusion of the Paris Pact;* James T. Shotwell, *War as an Instrument of National Policy;* John E. Stoner, *S. O. Levinson and the Pact of Paris.*

be appropriate to use the customary procedures of international adjudication. As a hypothetical example, a dispute over whether some particular action of State X was a violation of the pact would have to be decided on the basis of whether the act complained of was in fact "other than pacific" or a "recourse to war" within the meaning of the treaty. Since it was understood that warlike measures taken in self-defense were not forbidden by the pact, the plea of defensive necessity could be entered by State X and would have to be examined by the adjudicatory tribunal hearing the controversy. Furthermore, some statement in the *travaux preparatoires*, such as the British reservation of special interest in certain regions, might have to be interpreted.[35]

The real significance of the Pact of Paris, however, must be found in the broader question of its relation to and effect upon the basic principles of international law and organization. Specifically, to what extent did it modify previously existing rights and obligations of third states with respect to a nation having recourse to war? Clearly a party to the Pact of Paris could no longer use war as an instrument of national policy or seek the settlement of disputes by other than pacific means without violating the terms of a treaty with practically every other state in the world. The signing and ratification of, or adherence to, the pact by any state was *ipso facto* an assertion of national concern with reference to the settlement of any international dispute among the parties by nonpacific means and likewise constituted an admission that all the other parties had a similar interest in the question of whether that signatory or adherent would ever seek to achieve its national ends by recourse to war.

What would be the juridical consequences of a violation of the Pact of Paris? No specific sanctions and no procedure for dealing with a violator were included in the pact. Its brevity

[35] As a matter of fact, a dispute serious enough to provoke recourse to armed force would probably not be submitted to international adjudication—except under coercion. The hypothetical example is adopted merely as a device to state the questions which would arise in interpreting the legal application of the Pact of Paris to a specific controversy.

and generality were conceived by its authors to be among its chief advantages. The possibility of a violation was not even mentioned in the body of the pact. The preamble, however, stated that the signatories are "convinced" that "any signatory Power which shall hereafter seek to promote its national interests by resort to war should be denied the benefits furnished by this Treaty." Two points concerning the legal force of this clause might be raised: (a) are declaratory statements in the preamble of a treaty legally binding? and (b) if so, is the force of the declaration weakened by the fact that it does not provide that violators *lose* the "benefits of the Treaty," but only that the signatories are *convinced* that they *should?* Fortunately, the answer to these questions becomes practically unimportant when we consider that any contention that a violator of a treaty can continue to claim the benefit of its provisions would be immediately rejected as unsound and absurd.

It seems to be established that a state which violated the Pact of Paris automatically would release the other signatories from their promise to it not to have recourse to war and make itself subject to the general sanctions of international law for treaty violation. That is, a violation of the pact would involve a reversion to the *status quo ante* with respect to the legal right of the other signatories to go to war or to use nonpacific means of settlement as against the violator.[36] But it should be emphasized that the loss of the "benefits of the Treaty" would not be a mere cancellation of its provisions with respect to a signatory, such as that involved in the normal lapsing of any treaty. A breach of the pact would constitute an injury to all its signatories and thereby lay the violator open to reprisals—measures against which the act of violation had destroyed the defaulting state's legal defense. A nation which did not observe its obligations under the Pact of Paris would lose the advantages conferred by that instrument and in addition take upon itself the onus of treaty violation. Since reprisals may legitimately be

[36] The other signatories remain bound among themselves, and their obligations to the violator under other treaties might or might not be affected. Only the consequences of a violation of the Pact of Paris itself are under consideration here.

proportioned to the seriousness of a wrong suffered, it would
be open to third states to adopt a grave view of the consequences of a disturbance of the peace and to take any measures
appropriate and effective to curb the aggressor.

That the Pact of Paris was not conceived to be merely an
idle gesture is suggested by the subsequent development of
the principle of nonrecognition of acquisitions made by force
of arms.[37] When hostilities broke out between China and the
U.S.S.R. in 1929, communications were addressed to the two
governments, on the initiative of the United States, by thirty-
one signatories of the pact, expressing concern at the resort to
force and calling upon the disputants to settle their quarrel by
peaceful means.[38] Secretary of State Stimson said with respect
to this action that "this government regards the Pact of Paris
as a covenant which has profoundly modified the attitude of
the world toward peace and . . . this government intends to
shape its own policy accordingly."[39]

When the Chaco hostilities broke out between Bolivia and
Paraguay, the Pact of Paris had not been ratified by the former. However, nineteen American states asserted in a note
to the disputants that "the Chaco dispute is susceptible of a
peaceful solution" and that they would not recognize "any territorial arrangement of the controversy which has not been
obtained by peaceful means nor the validity of territorial acquisitions which may be obtained through occupation or conquest by force of arms."[40]

During the course of Sino-Japanese hostilities in Manchuria
the United States government formally notified both Japan and
China on January 7, 1932, that it would not recognize any
situation, treaty, or agreement which might be brought about
by means contrary to the covenant and obligations of the Pact
of Paris. On the following March 11 the Assembly of the
League of Nations unanimously adopted a resolution, with
Japan refraining from voting, declaring that "it is incumbent

[37] See Section 4 of this chapter.
[38] United States Department of State, *Press Releases*, December 7, 1929,
pp. 83-84.
[39] Same, 86-87.   [40] Same, August 6, 1932, pp. 100-101.

upon the Members of the League not to recognize any situation, treaty, or agreement which may be brought about by means contrary to the Covenant of the League of Nations or to the Pact of Paris."[41]

Secretary of State Stimson, in discussing the significance of the pact in his speech of August 8, 1932, said: "On its face it is a treaty containing definite promises. . . . As it stands, the only limitation against war is the right of self-defense. . . . From the day of its ratification . . . it has been the determined aim of the American Government . . . to insure that the Pact of Paris should become a living force in the world. . . . But now under the covenants of the Briand-Kellogg Pact such a conflict [that in Manchuria] becomes of concern to everybody connected with the Pact. All of the steps taken to enforce the treaty must be judged by this new situation."[42]

Also, it is of interest to note that the Budapest Articles of Interpretation, adopted by the International Law Association in 1934, affirmed that the pact was a multilateral law-making treaty and provided in part that

in the event of a violation of the Pact . . . by one signatory State against another, the other States may, without thereby committing a breach of the Pact or of any rule of International Law, do all or any of the following things:

(a) Refuse to admit the exercise by the State violating the Pact of belligerent rights, such as visit and search, blockade, etc.;

(b) Decline to observe towards the State violating the Pact the duties prescribed by International Law, apart from the Pact, for a neutral in relation to a belligerent;

(c) Supply the State attacked with financial or material assistance, including munitions of war;

(d) Assist with armed forces the State attacked.[43]

So much for the rights which third states signatory to the Pact of Paris acquired against a violator of its terms. There is, however, a further question, namely, what *obligations*, if any,

---

[41] Westel W. Willoughby, *The Sino-Japanese Controversy and the League of Nations*, 206, 300.

[42] Henry L. Stimson, *The Pact of Paris: Three Years of Development*, 5-7,10.

[43] International Law Association, *Briand-Kellogg Pact of Paris: Articles of Interpretation as Adopted by the Budapest Conference, 1934*, 63-64.

would third states acquire as a result of the breach of the pact? Or, was there a *legal duty* to apply differential treatment? There have been a large number of contentions to the effect that the Pact of Paris "ended neutrality" among its signatories. In 1928 David Hunter Miller wrote, "Following the Covenant, one of the consequences of this Treaty is that neutrality, in case of war, in the hitherto accepted sense of neutrality, is ended."[44]

In 1929 an article in the *American Journal of International Law* contained the statement, "To the extent, therefore, that the signatories and adherents to the Pact of Paris have really renounced war, they have of necessity renounced neutrality also, as neutrality, in its last analysis, is a co-function of the status of war."[45]

A noted British journalist wrote that "those Governments which had renounced war, by signing and ratifying the Briand-Kellogg Pact, really renounced at the same time their right to be neutral towards a war maker."[46]

Secretary Stimson in his speech of August 8, 1932, interpreted the pact as rendering obsolete the traditional notions of neutral rights and duties. He said, "War between nations was renounced by the signatories of the Briand-Kellogg Treaty. This means that it has become illegal throughout practically the entire world. It is no longer to be the source and subject of rights. It is no longer to be the principle around which the duties, the conduct, and the rights of nations revolve. It is an illegal thing."[47]

The Budapest Articles of Interpretation contained the statement that "the signatory States are not entitled to recognize as acquired *de jure* any territorial or other advantages acquired *de facto* by means of a violation of the Pact."[48]

[44] *The Peace Pact of Paris,* 132.
[45] Graham, "The Soviet Security Treaties," 347.
[46] Wickham Steed, *Vital Peace,* 197.
[47] *The Pact of Paris,* 4, 5; cp. Quincy Wright, "The Meaning of the Pact of Paris," *American Journal of International Law,* XXVII (1933), 39-61.
[48] International Law Association, 64.

Can it be assumed that a renunciation of war as an instrument of national policy and a covenant not to seek the solution of disputes by other than pacific means necessarily involved a renunciation of the right to be impartial if the undertaking was violated by another party to it?

The answer to this question is clearly in the negative. First, no stipulation that third states are bound to adopt measures against a violator was included in the text of the pact. This alone would be a conclusive point, since existing obligations and relationships persist unless modified by express agreement or necessary inference. Strict construction is to be placed on the allegation of new rights and duties not definitely set forth. Second, mandatory sanctions were not even considered as a possibility in the negotiations leading to the pact. There was no suggestion of adding to the obligations under the League Covenant and the Locarno agreements. When signatory states had insisted that each member must decide for itself the applicability of sanctions under the Covenant and had consistently rejected proposals to place such a decision with the Council, there could be no reason to anticipate that their attitude would be otherwise in connection with the Pact of Paris.

Finally, an automatic prohibition of the right to remain neutral was inconsistent with the basis on which the United States was willing to consider a general treaty for the renunciation of war. The whole conception and direction of the proposal was quite otherwise. Although the point was not raised during the negotiations, specific mention was made of it in a report from the Committee on Foreign Relations in connection with the consent to ratification by the United States Senate. Nothing in this report had the effect of a reservation to the pact, but with the United States outside the League and not risking membership in the world court, there could be no doubt that the following statement on record in the Senate and uncontradicted by the Executive was an accurate reflection of United States policy. The report made assurance twice (or thrice) sure in these words:

The committee further understands the treaty does not provide sanctions, express or implied. Should any signatory to the treaty or any nation adhering to the treaty violate the terms of the same, there is no obligation or commitment, express or implied, upon the part of any of the signers of the treaty to engage in punitive or coercive measures as against the nation violating the treaty. The effect of the violation of the treaty is to relieve the other signers of the treaty from any obligation under it with the nation thus violating the same.

In other words, the treaty does not, either expressly or impliedly, contemplate the use of force or coercive measures for its enforcement as against any nation violating it. It is a voluntary pledge upon the part of each nation that it will not have recourse to war except in self-defense, and that it will not seek settlement of its international controversies except through pacific means. And if a nation sees proper to disregard the treaty and violate the same, the effect of such action is to take it from under the benefits of the treaty and to relieve the other nations from any treaty relationship with the said power.[49]

Since the entire conception on the basis of which the pact was negotiated and adopted was that no provisions for sanctions were to be written into it, convincing presumptions are raised against any argument to the effect that all other signatories were legally bound to penalize a violator. To say that a state had renounced war as an instrument of national policy was by no means logically equivalent to saying that a state had abandoned its right to remain aloof if another party to the same renunciation of war broke its pledge.[50] There is no warrant in international law for depriving a nation of the option of ignoring the adverse breach of a treaty to which it is a party. In such a case a state is *entitled* to take appropriate reprisals for the wrong suffered, but it is not *legally obligated* to take such reprisals.

At this point one might say that the influence and authority of international law would suffer irreparable damage if states

[49] United States Congress, *Congressional Record*, 70th Cong., 2d Sess., 1730.

[50] Subject, of course, to the requirements of other treaties to which the states are parties. It might be argued that there is a duty to make a specific public condemnation of each breach of the Pact of Paris. For a discussion of this point, see Quincy Wright, "The Denunciation of Treaty Violators," *American Journal of International Law*, XXXII (1938), 526-35.

made a practice of ignoring breaches of the most solemn and important treaty pledges among themselves. It is quite obvious, and all too well illustrated by a series of deplorable events, that failure to halt aggression undertaken in violation of the Pact of Paris encouraged new breaches of that instrument and robbed it of all practical value. Still, the fact that disastrous consequences may follow an attitude of indifference does not read into the Pact of Paris the obligation to take definite measures against a state violating its pledge. Interpretation of the pact does not differ from that which prevailed with respect to Article 16 of the Covenant of the League of Nations, namely, that each state remained the judge of its own participation in adverse differential treatment of an aggressor.

This does not mean, however, that those who spoke of obligations to implement the Pact of Paris were wrong in their interpretation of that instrument. They were profoundly right in the sense that they were speaking of what must be done *if the pact was to be effective.* One may well say that it is inconceivable that a state which had signed the Pact of Paris in good faith and which had a genuine interest in the abolition of war as a legitimate technique of international intercourse would be neutral in the event of a violation and would refuse to avail itself of its legal right to make its concern effective. If international development were to follow principles upon which the pact was based, it would be necessary for all third states to take appropriate measures for the restraint of aggression, and the first step would be an unequivocal forsaking of the attitude of indifference to the methods by which any international dispute whatsoever is settled.

The fact that the pact did not contain sanctions is relatively unimportant. If third states directed their policy toward implementing the pact, adequate procedures had already been developed; if they were not sufficiently concerned in establishing the principle of pacific settlement, any treaty requirement might be avoided or ignored. There is a real distinction between a legal duty arising from the terms of a treaty, literally interpreted, and the prerequisites of action calculated to implement the principle upon which that treaty is based, but so far as practical action is concerned, they are brought into harmony whenever states take the most, not the least, effective measures they can to discriminate against any of their number having recourse to war.

The interpretation of the consequences of a renunciation of war has been done largely, if not entirely, by those who are anxious to see it observed. They have usually been concerned with the broader and more important question of the place of the Pact of Paris in the development of international organization. They have spoken not of the least that third states can do without violating the pact, but of what they must do if it is to have practical value and force. Nowhere is this assumption more clearly and forcibly stated than in Secretary Stimson's speech of August 8, 1932. He said:

So the entire central point from which the problem of war was viewed was changed. . . . The Briand-Kellogg Pact provides for no sanctions of force. . . . Its efficacy depends upon the will of the people of the world to make it effective. . . . We have recognized that its effectiveness depends upon the cultivation of the mutual fidelity and good faith of the group of nations which has become its signatories. Another consequence is that consultation between the signatories of the Pact when faced with the threat of invasion becomes inevitable. Any effective invocation of the power of world opinion postulates discussion and consultation.[51]

The real significance of the Pact of Paris, then, must be found in its function as a basis for the implementation of the techniques of peaceful settlement. The Pact of Paris provided a basis for permissive sanctions, that is to say, for adverse differential treatment of a signatory state having recourse to war as an instrument of national policy. For all practical purposes, no country could resort to war without violating a treaty with each and every other nation in the world. For the obligation of treaty observance there is the reciprocal right to have treaties observed by others. States may take appropriate measures to protect their rights, including the benefits promised them by

[51] *The Pact of Paris*, 4, 7, 11.

treaty. This doctrine is entirely adequate to include a case of a violation of the renunciation of war as a national policy. It offers a legal basis for asserting that an act of war in any part of the world *ipso facto* violates a vital national interest.

4. Nonrecognition as a Sanction

A significant form of modified application of the principle of concern is found in the device of nonrecognition, or the Stimson Doctrine as it was known from the American Secretary of State who enunciated it. On January 7, 1932, the United States government addressed to China and Japan an identic note containing this paragraph:

> In view of the present situation and of its own rights and obligations therein, the American Government deems it to be its duty to notify both the Government of the Chinese Republic and the Imperial Japanese Government that it cannot admit the legality of any situation *de facto* nor does it intend to recognize any treaty or agreement entered into between these governments, or agents thereof, which may impair the treaty rights of the United States or its citizens in China, including those which relate to the sovereignty, the independence or the territorial and administrative integrity of the Republic of China, or to the international policy relative to China, commonly known as the Open Door Policy; and that it does not intend to recognize any situation, treaty, or agreement which may be brought about by means contrary to the covenants and obligations of the Pact of Paris of August 27, 1928, to which treaty both China and Japan, as well as the United States, are parties.[52]

The doctrine of nonrecognition was applied to the Sino-Japanese dispute by the League of Nations, in terms of Article 10 of the Covenant by a Council resolution of February 16, 1932, and in terms of the Covenant of the League and the Pact of Paris by an Assembly resolution of March 11, 1932. It was also applied in connection with the Chaco dispute in South America.

[52] United States Department of State, *Press Releases*, January, 1932.

The Stimson Doctrine gave a new application to the concepts of recognition and nonrecognition in international law. Historically, recognition had been associated with the act or process by which a new state or government was accepted into and became a participant in the family of nations. The term was also used to refer to the acceptance by third states of a new treaty or a new international legal situation. This, however, was by no means a settled branch of international law. Some of the questions involved in the traditional concepts were: Is recognition constitutive or declaratory? Does a state become an international personality and a subject of international law by virtue of its recognition, or does recognition merely accept a fact which already existed? Is the act of recognition legal or political, or both? Is the distinction between *de jure* and *de facto* recognition legitimate? Is it permissible for third states to grant or withhold recognition as a matter of policy? Does recognition involve or imply some degree of approval, or is it equivalent to a mere admission of the existence of facts? What of the distinctions between the recognition of states, of governments, of treaties, of belligerency or insurgency, and of other situations and facts? Could recognition be conditional? Is it revocable?[53]

A re-examination of these and other questions involved in the concept of recognition would amount to a long and controversial detour so far as this study is concerned. It is sufficient to indicate that these controversies exist, as a matter of perspective, since the relevant question for the present purpose is one of the Stimson Doctrine as a method of implementing the principle of concern. From this point of view, certain conclusions become obvious. First, the simple declaratory theory of recognition would be abandoned in favor of the

---

[53] It is instructive to review the discussions, by Baty, Borchard, Brown, Fenwick, Garner, Kelsen, and Wright, published in the *American Journal of International Law* during the period 1932-1944. See XXVI (1932), 342-48; XXVII (1933), 509-16; XXX (1936), 377-81, 679-94; XXXV (1941), 605-17; XXXVI (1942), 106-11; XXXVIII (1944), 448-52. For an analysis of the subject, with the texts of pertinent documents, see Chesney Hill, "Recent Policies of Non-Recognition."

constitutive theory that a state becomes a subject of international law only through recognition. The new element would be a modification of the criteria of eligibility for recognition.

In the second place, nonrecognition as a sanction to implement the principle of concern requires maintenance of the distinction between *de facto* and *de jure* situations. Recognition cannot be made equivalent to an admission of existence. Recognition becomes a matter of official cognizance, of acceptance as valid on the basis of designated criteria. By way of example, an analogy may be drawn with the practice of British and American courts. When an attempt is made to submit alleged facts which are inadmissible under the rules of evidence, the courts do not deny their existence but merely exclude them from the notice of the court. The issue is not the ultimate truth or falsity of the allegations, but whether their nature and presentation warrants admission to the purview of the court. Recognition in this sense means "acceptance for a purpose." On the other hand, it would not mean approval or disapproval. Mere existence is not conclusive as to legal recognition, and the latter does not necesarily imply endorsement. It seems apparent that those who deny any validity to the distinction between *de facto* and *de jure* recognition are able to reach this result only by making recognition equivalent to the admission that "what exists, exists." However, it often happens that the scope of judicial cognizance is not coterminous with the raw facts. That the crux of the matter lies in the acceptance of a state, rather than in deciding whether or not it exists, seems to be supported by the statement in Moore's *Digest of International Law,* "Recognition, says Rivier, is the assurance given to a new state that it will be permitted to hold its place or rank, in the character of an independent political organism, in the society of nations. The rights and attributes of sovereignty belong to it independently of all recognition, but it is only after it has been recognized that it is assured of exercising them."[54]

[54] Vol. I, 72.

A distinction between *de facto* and *de jure* recognition implies a test of legitimacy. The mere fact of existing or even of exercising actual authority is not sufficient to call forth immediate recognition of a new state or a new government. Under the theory of absolute monarchy the principle of legitimacy in the form of the hereditary right of a dynasty precluded any need for a doctrine of recognition. As the concept of popular sovereignty became important, the doctrine of recognition developed.[55] From the French Revolution through the Holy Alliance the defenders of the *status quo* in Europe put the recognition of governments to the test of their freedom from the taint of revolution. The better right of the existing (monarchic) form of government was asserted. The *de facto* theory countered the argument from legitimacy with the idea that any government which could establish itself in fact should be admitted to the society of nations. It was natural that the United States supported the *de facto* interpretation (except for the Civil War period) until the time of Woodrow Wilson's return to a test of legitimacy in the criterion of establishment according to constitutional means. Evidence of popular support was added to the requirements of actual control, reasonable stability, and a capacity for executing obligations. The Stimson Doctrine specifically added a test of legitimacy which excluded situations[56] created by other than pacific means. In cases of aggression a better right of the victim was asserted, even though the aggression might appear to be successful *de facto*. Compliance with the "covenants and obligations" of the Pact of Paris became a requirement for the recognition of the

[55] See Taylor Cole, "Recognition, International," *Encyclopedia of the Social Sciences*, XIII, 165-68.

[56] A general term is used here deliberately. Some of the analyses (for example, Hill) make much of distinctions between the recognition of states, governments, treaties, situations, etc. These distinctions are valid, but it must be remembered that the Manchurian situation involved questions of the recognition of a new state (Manchukuo), a new government, changes in multilateral treaties (Pact of Paris, Covenant of the League, Nine-Power Treaty), change in the territory of an existing state (China) and title to a portion of it, and the question of whether the fighting amounted to belligerency or insurgency (Japan alleging that Manchukuo was established by an indigenous separatist movement).

legitimacy and legal validity of changes in international relationships.

In the third place, the Stimson Doctrine involved the use of recognition as a policy, not as merely a matter of legal status arising from a condition of fact. Nonrecognition would be a sanction for use against aggression. In a sense, recognition has always involved policy determinations in that existing states do not have the legal duty of granting recognition. They have a decision to make. Under the *de facto* concept it is a decision whether a new state or government has actually established itself. Any test of legitimacy, of course, involves policy considerations over and above this. It is a matter of policy when one or more nations refuse recognition to any state or government born of revolution, or to one not based upon popular support, or to one which refuses to pay its debts. Likewise, it is a matter of policy, not legal duty, to refuse recognition to the "fruits of aggression." The Stimson Doctrine was not the first policy of nonrecognition against the use of force. The theory of dynastic legitimacy invoked it against changes made by popular revolution. The Wilsonian theory used it against seizures of power contrary to constitutional means. The Stimson Doctrine extended the theory to the external relations of states. Aggression against established dynasties, against constitutional governments, and against other states have been successively brought within the scope of a policy of nonrecognition. The Stimson Doctrine extended a principle designed for protection of the existing intrastate regime from forcible change to protection of the existing interstate situation from the same form of attack. A concept historically applied largely[57] to change of governments within states was extended to the legal relations between states.

Thus, the Stimson Doctrine involved a concept of recognition as constitutive, in that legal relationships depend upon

[57] When recognition has been based on a test of legitimacy, it has usually been concerned with either a revolutionary change of government within the same state or with a rebellion attempting to form a new state and government in a portion of the former state's territory.

recognition; as implying a distinction between *de facto* and *de jure* situations, with a test of legitimacy; and as a sanction for the implementation of policy, as well as a procedure for the determination of legal relationships.

On the basis of a new interpretation of the concept of recognition the Stimson Doctrine tended to establish or strengthen three propositions in international law.[58] First, *de facto* occupation of territory gives no title. It has usually been held that conquest alone does not give title, but that there must be confirmation by subsequent treaty, recognition of third states, or prescription. The policy of nonrecognition would be a barrier to acquisition of title, especially when a large number of states have a treaty right in the maintenance of the *status quo* in the disputed territory. There would be a new impediment to the completion of title after conquest in that a presumption against the legally effective transfer of territory by force would be erected.

Second, treaties contrary to the rights of third states are void. Traditionally, there has been a tendency to hold that such treaties are voidable at the discretion of the injured state, or at least that reparation is due for nonperformance of the original obligation. This principle would be followed under the Stimson Doctrine. The Pact of Paris is of significance at this point. By it, practically every state in the world acquired a vested interest in the maintenance of peace. It became impossible for any nation to resort to war or attempt nonpacific methods of settlement without violating a treaty with every other state. Therefore, changes made without the consent— the "recognition"—of third states would be void. Changes must be accepted to be valid.

Third, treaties made under duress, that is by nonpacific means, may be considered void. This would establish a general principle of international law, based upon the argument that duress is equivalent to nonpacific measures and that its use would violate the treaty rights of all other states.

[58] Quincy Wright, "The Stimson Note of January 7, 1932," *American Journal of International Law*, XXVI (1932), 342-48.

The main significance of the Stimson Doctrine for the principle of concern was that it made the validity of territorial and political changes dependent upon the attitude of third states toward the legitimacy of the methods used in effecting the changes. It expressed the concern of the international community in the existence and settlement of disputes among its members. In the words of Sir John Fischer Williams, "The novelty of the recent doctrine of Mr. Stimson and the League consists precisely in this—that it extends the necessity or opportunity of 'recognition' to cases in which it has not hitherto been supposed that any claim was addressed to the members of the international community and makes the rightfulness of action taken depend on the attitude of third Powers. This is to endow the members of the international community and third Powers with a new and important prerogative."[59]

Historically, a state always had a legitimate complaint if its treaty rights were violated. The Stimson Doctrine extended this in three ways. First, the network of multilateral treaties was much more extensive than formerly, involving in the Manchurian case the Covenant of the League, the Pact of Paris, and the Nine-Power Treaty. It was therefore much more difficult to make unilateral, or even bilateral, changes without violating one or more treaties with a large number of third states. Second, the Stimson Doctrine contemplated a degree of co-ordination in the attitude of third states. Its expression would then be a group or concerted affair, and not entirely a matter of each nation protecting its own national interests individually. This idea was not new, as witness the Concert of Europe, but it would be extended and strengthened. Third, more emphasis was placed on the methods used to effect a change rather than exclusively on the specific territorial and political changes being accomplished. Objections to treaty violation no longer were confined to this or that substantive change, but could include any change brought about by certain proscribed methods. There was a basis in international

[59] Grotius Society, *Transactions*, XVIII (1933), 113.

law and organization for asserting that states had a vested interest in the maintenance of peace.

This change of emphasis and extension of the concern of third states with international conflict is well illustrated by a comparison between the attitude of the United States toward a Sino-Japanese dispute in 1915 and that expressed by the Stimson Doctrine. In the former case, Secretary of State Bryan's note of May 11, 1915, relative to the Twenty-One Demands made upon China by Japan, stated that the United States "cannot recognize any agreement or undertaking which has been entered into or which may be entered into between the Governments of Japan and China, impairing the treaty rights of the United States and its citizens in China, the political or territorial integrity of the Republic of China, or the international policy relative to China commonly known as the open door policy."[60]

The above quotation was similar, and in part identical, with a portion of the Stimson note of January 7, 1932. But there were two differences, both significant in relation to the principle of concern. The statement of nonrecognition in the Stimson note was preceded by an indication that the United States "cannot admit the legality of any situation *de facto*," thus challenging Japanese action on the basis of law as well as policy. The other significant difference was that the Stimson note added a statement of intention not to recognize any situation, treaty, or agreement brought about contrary to the Pact of Paris. The Bryan note of 1915 asserted the national interests and policies of the United States; the Stimson note of 1932 asserted the same national interests and policies, plus a demand for observance of the Pact of Paris. This was clear evidence of an acceptance by the United States of a concern in the method by which international disputes are settled.

The intent of this discussion of the Stimson Doctrine has been to ascertain whether it represented an acceptance of the principle of concern and, if so, to what extent. However, the question of the functional effectiveness of nonrecognition as a

[60] United States *Foreign Relations* (1915), 146.

sanction should not be entirely neglected. Certain conclusions are evident. First, the policy of nonrecognition was not effective enough to get the Japanese out of China. Second, there was not sufficient time for the implications of a new concept of recognition and nonrecognition to work themselves out. It was seven years and a few months from the announcement of the Stimson Doctrine to the outbreak of World War II. The final test of a doctrine of nonrecognition would be its implications for the doctrine of prescription. That, by definition, takes more than seven years. What would happen if political and territorial changes brought about by nonpacific means were stabilized *de facto* over a long period of time?

The practical effects of the nonrecognition of a new nation or government would lie in the difficulties of travel, commerce, status of nationals before the courts of third states, and the like. The unrecognized country would be unable to protect its nationals abroad in the normal manner, to secure respect for its flag, to maintain regular diplomatic relations, or to establish consular offices. On the other hand, third states would also suffer inconveniences from the continuation of such a situation. It seems clear that nonrecognition as a sanction would be effective only to the extent that a recalcitrant state could be brought to terms by a combination of comparatively minor inconveniences, appeal to public opinion, and moral suasion. This is not enough for a powerful and determined aggressor. In effect, the doctrine of nonrecognition represents an attempt to restrain aggression without the use of forcible means. Collective application of the policy of nonrecognition would be important. If all or nearly all third states concurred in this attitude, the difficulties for an unrecognized nation (or government) and its nationals would be greatly increased. If opinion and moral suasion, as evidenced by the policies of third states, were universal or nearly so, their force would be greatly enhanced. On the other hand, adoption of such a policy by only a few nations would minimize the inconveniences suffered and would reflect a divided world opinion and a narrower basis for moral suasion.

One of the most telling criticisms of a policy of nonrecognition is that it threatens to leave a gap between the law and the facts. The Stimson Doctrine would not be effective as a sanction if it meant merely ignoring obvious facts. This would discredit, not strengthen, the law. What the law cannot effectively control or prohibit, it must recognize in the interest of order and stability. "We shall do nothing—except administer a little opium to our mental and moral vigour—by saying that war and conquest, while we allow them to take place, produce results which are invalid in law."[61]

This would seem to be a conclusive criticism against a policy of nonrecognition unless that policy, alone or in conjunction with other measures, could prevent in fact the situation forbidden in law. A disapproved change must either be eliminated or eventually accepted. A doctrine of nonrecognition, by refusing to accept the actual situation and by putting difficulties in the way of international intercourse, might further disturb rather than stabilize international relations. In principle, the Stimson Doctrine can be defended only on the basis of assuming that its implications can be made effective. Refusal to ignore facts is valueless, or worse; but refusal to accept a state of facts as a step in securing a change in them is of great value if the means exist for making the policy effective in practice.

Finally, a question may be raised about the implications of a policy of nonrecognition for the problem of peaceful change. Would the Stimson Doctrine refuse to recognize changes made by force while sanctioning a *status quo* maintained by force? Prohibition of nonpacific methods carries with it an increased necessity for the development of effective pacific methods. But such a prohibition can be based only upon a concern of the group in the existence and settlement of conflicts among its members. This partial control of the methods of settlement offers a basis for the elaboration of permissible means as a society develops.

[61] John Fischer Williams, "Sovereignty, Seisin and the League," *British Yearbook of International Law*, VII (1936), 42.

5. The Inter-American System

The various trends in the modified application of the principle of concern, together with various outbreaks of international violence, emphasized the desirability of co-ordinating and implementing the general obligations of peaceful settlement among the American republics. Accordingly, the Seventh International Conference of American States, meeting at Montevideo, Uruguay, in December, 1933, turned its attention to this problem. As a result the conference adopted a resolution inviting the adherence of each of the American states to five instruments for the maintenance of peace which, the conference felt, "if coordinated and converted into obligations enforced in every country of the American Continent, would suffice to prevent the crime of war and the disastrous consequences of every kind which it entails for the present and future of all nationalities."[62]

The five peace instruments to be co-ordinated were the Treaty for Avoiding and Preventing Conflicts, concluded at Santiago, Chile, in 1923 and known as the "Gondra Treaty"; the Pact of Paris; the Conciliation Convention, signed in Washington in 1929; the Inter-American Arbitration Treaty of the same year; and the Argentine Anti-War Treaty, signed in Rio de Janeiro in 1933.[63] Of this group, the Gondra Treaty of 1923 and the two Washington conventions of 1929 provided for procedures of inquiry, conciliation, and arbitration, and contained no references to discriminatory treatment between disputing states. The Pact of Paris has previously been discussed.[64]

[62] Seventh International Conference of American States, *Final Act*, 20.

[63] Same. The Fifth International Conference of American States, meeting at Santiago in 1923, had also adopted a resolution recommending "that the Governments adhere to the Conventions of The Hague of 1907, and to the subsequent Conventions which limit military hostilities, fix the usages of warfare and the rights and duties of neutrals, and thus . . . tend to render the Positive International Law of the American Nations with regard to measures which mitigate the horrors of war and in general, with regard to the law of warfare" (*Verbatim Record of the Plenary Sessions*, II, 389). The Havana conference of 1928 adopted a resolution condemning aggression.

[64] Section 3.

The Argentine Anti-War Treaty, signed at Rio de Janeiro on October 10, 1933, by Argentina, Brazil, Chile, Mexico, Paraguay, and Uruguay, condemned wars of aggression among themselves and with other states, and declared that the settlement of controversies of any kind which arose among the parties should be settled only "by pacific means which have the sanction of international law."[65] Territorial arrangements not obtained by pacific means, as well as the validity of the occupation or acquisition of territories brought about by force of arms, were not to be recognized. Article 3 of the treaty provided that

in case of non-compliance by any State engaged in a dispute, with the obligations contained in the foregoing articles, the contracting States undertake to make every effort for the maintenance of peace. To that end they will adopt in their character as neutrals a common and solidary attitude; they will exercise the political, juridical, or economic means authorized by international law; they will bring the influence of public opinion to bear but will in no case resort to intervention either diplomatic or armed; subject to the attitude that may be incumbent on them by virtue of other collective treaties to which such States are signatories.[66]

At the same conference the Mexican government submitted a Peace Code, Chapter I of which contained statements practically identical with Articles 1 to 3 of the Argentine Anti-War Treaty. The conference voted to submit the Peace Code through the channel of the Pan-American Union to the consideration of its member governments.[67]

There was also concluded at the Montevideo conference a Convention on the Rights and Duties of States, which provided in Article II that "the contracting states definitely establish as

[65] Article 1. For the text, see United States Department of State, *Treaty Series*, No. 906.

[66] Same. The remainder of the treaty provided for a procedure of reconciliation.

[67] Seventh International Conference of American States, 6-63. Chapter I of the Peace Code offered a definition of aggression and contained an express declaration against resort to armed force for the collection of contractual debts. The remaining articles provided for conciliation and the creation of a permanent commission, arbitration, and the establishment of an American Court of International Justice (pp. 62-85).

a rule of their conduct the precise obligation not to recognize territorial acquisitions or special advantages which have been obtained by force whether this consists in the employment of arms, in threatening diplomatic representations, or in any other effective coercive measures."[68]

The conference also named the "Determination of the Aggressor and Condition of Neutrals" as a subject to be submitted as a base of discussion for the International Commission of American Jurists.[69]

The integration and co-ordination of Pan-American peace instruments was continued at the Inter-American Conference for the Maintenance of Peace, which met at Buenos Aires in December, 1936. Although this conference took place after the period of modified application of the principle of concern, properly speaking, it is considered here because of its intimate relation to preceding measures and because only in this way can the attempt at integration of an inter-American peace system be viewed in perspective. At the outset the conference approved a resolution reaffirming the invitation to the American countries which had not already done so to adhere to or ratify the five peace instruments recommended by the Montevideo conference.[70]

A Convention for the Maintenance, Preservation, and Reestablishment of Peace, concluded at the conference, provided that in the event of a menace to the peace of the American republics the signatories to the Pact of Paris and the Argentine Anti-War Treaty would consult with other governments of the American republics, and that in the event of war or a "virtual state of war" between American republics the states represented at the conference would undertake mutual consultations. In the event of an international war outside America

[68] Same, 192-93. The next article provided that "the present Convention shall not affect obligations previously entered into by the High Contracting Parties by virtue of international agreements."

[69] Same, 113.

[70] Inter-American Conference for the Maintenance of Peace, *Final Act* (Buenos Aires, 1936), 7. The recommendation was extended to include the Additional Protocol to the General Convention of Inter-American Conciliation of 1929.

which might menace the peace of the American republics, such consultation would also take place.[71]

The Buenos Aires conference also approved a Declaration of Principles of Inter-American Solidarity and Co-operation which proscribed territorial conquest and stated that no acquisition made through violence would be recognized, condemned intervention by one state in the internal or external affairs of another, asserted the illegality of the forcible collection of pecuniary debts, and finally, provided that "any difference or dispute between the American nations, whatever its nature or origin, shall be settled by the methods of conciliation, or unrestricted arbitration, or through operation of international justice."[72]

Another resolution of the conference referred the Mexican Peace Code to a Committee of Experts on the Codification of International Law, and a fourth recommended that the American states not members of the League of Nations but parties to the Pact of Paris and the Argentine Anti-War Treaty "and any other similar agreements signed in the future" co-operate with the League of Nations in the prevention of war and the pacific settlement of international conflicts whenever the respective legal systems of such states permitted.[73]

A precise statement of the duties and obligations with respect to international violence resulting from this group of conventions could be only provisional and speculative, for two reasons: (a) the task of co-ordinating the various instruments was not completed and (b) the nature of certain of the textual provisions involved was such that their specific application could not be stated with any degree of exactness.

Obvious difficulties inhere in the coexistence of several multilateral conventions for the maintenance of peace, the stipulations of which are not identical, although directed toward the same object, and none of which has been accepted by all the

[71] United States Department of State, *Treaty Series*, No. 922. Paraguay, upon signing the convention, made a reservation with respect to its "peculiar international position as regards the League of Nations" (p. 5).

[72] Same, 16.

[73] Same, 16-17. The delegations of the United States and Costa Rica abstained from voting on the fourth resolution.

states concerned. One party to a conflict might be bound by one treaty or combination of treaties, with the other party bound by a different treaty or combination. Likewise, each party would be bound by different treaties or combinations with respect to the several third states. The various "combinations and permutations" would logically be complex, and the possibilities of playing one treaty against another are apparent. Efforts for maintenance of peace among the American republics might be effectively co-ordinated by practical international statesmanship availing itself of such techniques as might be appropriate, but it is nevertheless true that the conventional basis for effective action was not integrated.[74]

This lack of complete co-ordination among peace instruments is, of course, of definitely secondary importance, provided that each state is bound by *some* international agreement not to resort to hostilities and that the violation of *any* such agreement is conceived to be an occasion for the fullest possible use of the existing machinery for the maintenance of peace. The noncoincidence of adherents to the various conventions is a minor difficulty if those conventions function as supplements to each other; it is a serious problem if they are manipulated so as to interfere with each other.

The second source of difficulty in appraising the place of the principle of differential treatment in the movement for the implementation of peace among the American republics is uncertainty as to the force of some of the substantive obligations undertaken, particularly in the provisions of the Argentine Anti-War Treaty. It is clear that this convention required non-recognition of territorial arrangements brought about by the

[74] The following instruments for the maintenance of peace were relevant to the application of the principle of differential treatment to American international organization: (1) League of Nations Covenant; (2) Pact of Paris; (3) Argentine Anti-War Treaty; (4) Convention on the Rights and Duties of States; (5) Convention for the Maintenance, Preservation, and Re-establishment of Peace. As of April 1, 1938, the different combinations by which the various American republics were bound were as follows: All five: Colombia, Cuba, Dominican Republic, Ecuador, Honduras, Mexico, Nicaragua; 1, 2, 3, 4: Chile, Guatemala; 1, 2, 3, 5: Venezuela; 1, 2, 3: Haiti, Panama, Peru; 1, 3, 4, 5: El Salvador; 1, 3: Argentina, Bolivia, Uruguay; 2, 3, 4, 5: Brazil, United States; 2, 4: Costa Rica; 2: Paraguay.

use of violence; moreover, an obligation upon the parties to consult in the event of a breach of Articles 1 and 2 was indisputably implicit in the convention, since independent and unco-ordinated national policies could scarcely result in a "common and solidary attitude."

The doubtful points related specifically to three qualifying expressions in Article 3. It was provided that in the event of noncompliance with Articles 1 and 2 by any nation engaged in a dispute, the contracting states would adopt a common attitude "in their character as neutrals." The meaning of the word "neutrals" in this connection was obscure. If it was used in the traditional sense of impartiality between parties to a conflict, regardless of the merits of the case, it was not consistent with the condemnation of aggression by the pact; if it merely meant "nonparticipants" or "third states," its use in this particular place was superfluous. It might have been used to connote that the measures taken for the maintenance of peace were to fall short of actual participation in the controversy, that abstention from involvement in hostilities against a violator of the pact was to be a fundamental rule of any action based upon a "common and solidary attitude."

Article 3 then stated that the contracting parties "will exercise the political, juridical, or economic means authorized by international law; they will bring the influence of public opinion to bear but will in no case resort to intervention either diplomatic or armed." Even if it be assumed that there would be agreement upon what means were "authorized by international law," it would seem rather difficult clearly to distinguish intervention from "exercising political, juridical, or economic means" and "bringing the influence of public opinion to bear." If third states interested themselves in a conflict to the extent of applying various political, juridical, or economic measures against one of the participants in that conflict, they would seem to be "intervening" within the traditional interpretation of that term. No doubt the present qualification might be taken as a guarantee against coercion of any American republic with respect to its domestic affairs and as a pledge that third states would not, under the guise of collective action for the maintenance of peace, take sides in a "private war" for their own national aggrandizement. But at any rate, it must be admitted that obligations to take "political, juridical, or economic means" without "resorting to intervention" were open to grave difficulties of interpretation and application.

A third difficulty lay in the qualifying clause, "subject to the attitude that may be incumbent on them by virtue of other collective treaties to which such states are signatories." The Covenant of the League immediately comes to mind. Some of the signatories of the Argentine Anti-War Treaty were members of the League; others were not. What would happen to their "solidary attitude" if, for example, the League should attempt to apply sanctions? The possibility of adoption of a policy of "isolation" by the United States and the Latin American predilection for withdrawing from the League were sufficient warning against optimistic reliance on enthusiastic co-operation with any action which the League might take. The American system of collective security might be able to function effectively without the support of non-American states. But this assumption, too, is undependable. It would not be correct to assert that the qualification with respect to "other collective treaties" would necessarily produce an impasse, but it would be equally incorrect to contend that it did not afford a real possibility of doing so.

In short, a consideration of the obligations imposed by the Pact of Paris and various other conventions for the implementation of peace leads to the conclusion that a judgment of their implications for international law and organization could not be derived from their texts alone, but had to be based also upon their actual functional interpretation in relevant situations. This was true because many of their stipulations were permissive rather than obligatory, the force of several important qualifying expressions was uncertain, and some of the basic provisions were stated in terms of general principles, the detailed applications of which were not susceptible to precise delimitation in advance.

CHAPTER FIVE

Disintegration

THE FOURTH and last phase of international organization for the control of conflict during the period 1919-1939 was characterized by disintegration. The attempt at modified application of the principle of concern was unsuccessful. And the only alternative to its success was complete failure to incorporate the principle into international law and organization as a basis for the control of international conflict. The outbreak of World War II marked that failure. Since the phase of disintegration was so acutely and universally apparent, no extended discussion is necessary to establish its occurrence. Accordingly, this chapter will be limited to a recapitulation of the major trends in organized attitudes toward international conflict.

There is some problem in dating the period of disintegration of the system of collective security between the two World Wars. Important disruptive factors had been evident from the beginning. As in the case of the trends of acceptance, limitation, and modified application, the phase of disintegration was a matter more of emphasis than of an exclusive characteristic. From this point of view, the period of disintegration commenced as attempts at modified application were shown to be ineffectual. This process occurred gradually over a period of time. The beginning of the end might be set as 1931, when the Manchurian incident launched a cycle of major aggressions which disrupted the League of Nations and the system built around it. On the other hand, major attempts at modified application occurred during 1932-1933. The two years from

1931 to 1933 were really a time of overlapping between modified application and disintegration, with the eventual development of the latter in inverse proportion to the success of the
former. Since the object of this study is to trace the pattern
of international organization vis-à-vis international conflict, it
seems preferable on the whole to date the phase of disintegration as beginning in 1933. In this year the collective attitude
toward the Sino-Japanese conflict became definitive by virtue
of acceptance of the Lytton Commission's report and the Assembly resolution based upon it. Although the conflict had
started in 1931, the decisive test of the collective ability to
deal with it came in 1933 with the question of the League's
effectiveness, or lack of it, in bringing the situation under
control on the basis of its obligations, expressed attitude, and
the findings of its Commission of Enquiry. In other words the
interest of this study lies in the failure to deal with the conflict
rather than in the event as such. Acceptance of the date 1933
is reinforced by the further fact that the Nazi government
came to power and Germany gave notice of its withdrawal
from the League of Nations at this time.

1. The Incidents

The principle of concern during the phase of disintegration
will now be examined briefly from the perspective of the organized collective attitude toward three incidents of international
conflict—one in the Far East, one in South America, and one
involving a major European power.

(a) The Sino-Japanese Conflict

On the night of September 18-19, 1931, Japanese and Chinese
forces clashed near Mukden in Manchuria. Japanese troops
occupied Mukden. On September 19, the Council of the
League heard statements concerning the incidents by Chinese
and Japanese representatives. Hostilities continued to spread

in Manchuria, and on September 21 China appealed to the Council under Article 11 of the Covenant.[1] On the next day the Council authorized its President to appeal to the two governments to refrain from any act which might aggravate the situation or prejudice the peaceful settlement of the problem. Chinese and Japanese representatives were also to be consulted on means for the withdrawal of their respective troops. The Council decided to transmit records of its proceedings to the United States, and on September 24 the latter expressed "whole-hearted sympathy" with the attitude of the Council. On September 29 the President of the Council reported a Japanese statement that the withdrawal of its forces was proceeding. On the next day, September 30, the Council adopted a resolution which, after noting the replies of the two governments concerned, requested them to do all in their power to hasten the restoration of normal relations and to keep the Council fully informed.[2]

Hostilities continued to spread, however, and on October 13 the Council reconvened at the request of China. Upon invitation the United States sent a representative to the meeting of the Council to consider the situation in relation to the Pact of Paris. On October 17 seven states represented on the Council sent an identical note to the governments of China and Japan calling their attention to the provisions of that pact, and especially to Article 2. The United States government sent a similar note shortly afterward. This note was based upon the principle that "A threat of war, wherever it may arise, is of profound concern to the whole world."[3]

On October 24 a draft resolution fixing a date for the withdrawal of Japanese forces was lost in the Council by the adverse vote of Japan. The Japanese military operations in Manchuria continued to develop, and measures for the reorganization of the civil administration in Manchuria were undertaken under Japanese auspices. At its meeting in November and

[1] For the Sino-Japanese conflict, see Westel W. Willoughby, *The Sino-Japanese Controversy and the League of Nations;* United States Department of State, *Press Releases*, November 20, 27, 1937.
[2] Willoughby, 71-72.   [3] Same, 109.

December, 1931, the Council decided to appoint a Commission of Enquiry "to study on the spot and to report to the Council on any circumstance which, affecting international relations, threatens to disturb peace between China and Japan, or the good understanding between them, upon which peace depends."[4] Direct negotiations between the two parties and military arrangements were excluded from the terms of reference of the commission. The United States government indicated its gratification at this decision, stating, "This country is concerned that the methods employed in this settlement shall, in harmony with the obligations of the treaties to which we are parties, be made in a way which shall not endanger the peace of the world and that the result shall not be the result of military pressure."[5] On January 7, 1932, the United States announced its policy of nonrecognition.

On January 25, 1932, the Council resumed consideration of the dispute. By this time the hostilities had spread to Shanghai. On January 29 China made a new appeal under Articles 10, 11, and 15 of the Covenant. The Council requested the designation of consuls at Shanghai to act as a committee to report on the hostilities there and also endorsed mediation by the American, British, French, and Italian governments. On February 12 China asked the Council to refer the dispute to the Assembly under Article 15, paragraph 9, of the Covenant. On February 16 the members of the Council other than China and Japan addressed to the Japanese government an urgent appeal calling attention to Article 10 of the Covenant and stating that "no infringement of the territorial integrity and no change in the political independence of any Member of the League brought about in disregard of that article ought to be recognized as valid and effectual by Members of the League."[6]

The Council referred the dispute to the Assembly on February 19, and a Special Assembly was convened on March 3. The next day the Assembly adopted a resolution calling for the cessation of hostilities at Shanghai and recommending negotiations between Chinese and Japanese representatives, with the

4 Same, 178.   5 Same, 187.   6 Same, 240.

assistance of states having special interests there. The United
States government instructed its military authorities at Shanghai to co-operate. An armistice was finally signed in May. In
the meantime, the situation in Manchuria was progressing, the
declaration of independence of "Manchukuo" having been published on February 18.

The Assembly continued its examination of the dispute and
adopted on March 11, 1932, a resolution asserting a policy of
nonrecognition, declaring that "it is incumbent upon the Members of the League of Nations not to recognize any situation,
treaty or agreement which may be brought about by means
contrary to the Covenant of the League of Nations or to the
Pact of Paris."[7] The same resolution provided for the constitution of a Committee of Nineteen which would report to the
Assembly on the cessation of hostilities and withdrawal of
Japanese forces at Shanghai; follow the execution of resolutions adopted earlier by the Council; endeavor to prepare an
agreed settlement of the dispute; propose, if necessary, that the
Assembly request an advisory opinion from the Permanent
Court of International Justice; prepare, if necessary, the draft
of a report recommending a settlement under Article 15, paragraph 4, of the Covenant; propose any urgent measure needed;
and submit a progress report. The United States government
on March 12 expressed its gratification at this resolution of
the Assembly and especially at its adoption of the doctrine of
nonrecognition.

The report of the Commission of Enquiry was completed on
September 4, 1932, and published in the various capitals on
October 2. The findings of the commission rejected the Japanese contentions of self-defense and of a spontaneous independence movement in Manchuria.

The Japanese government asked for at least six weeks in
which to study the report. The Council heard the observations
of the Chinese and Japanese representatives at its meeting of
November 21-23 and voted to transmit the report to the Assembly, which referred it to the Committee of Nineteen with

[7] Same, 300.

instructions to draw up and submit proposals of settlement. In connection with this task, the committee submitted to the Chinese and Japanese governments draft resolutions under the conciliatory procedure required by Article 15, paragraph 3, of the Covenant. The two parties were at wide variance in their suggestions, and the Committee of Nineteen was able neither to find a basis for agreement between the governments nor to secure Japanese acceptance of any conciliatory procedure which the committee would be in a position to endorse. The committee then prepared a report, with its recommendations, and submitted it to the Assembly, which adopted it on February 24, 1933. The Assembly also adopted the findings of the Commission on Enquiry as follows:

Without excluding the possibility that, on the night of September 18-19, 1931, the Japanese officers on the spot may have believed that they were acting in self-defense, the Assembly cannot regard as measures of self-defense the military operations carried out on that night by the Japanese troops at Mukden and other places in Manchuria. Nor can the military measures of Japan as a whole, developed in the course of the dispute, be regarded as measures of self-defense. Moreover, the adoption of measures of self-defense does not exempt a state from complying with the provisions of Article 12 of the Covenant.

Since September 18, 1931, the activities of the Japanese military authorities, in civil as well as in military matters, have been marked by essentially political considerations. The progressive military occupation of the Three Eastern Provinces removed in succession all the important towns in Manchuria from the control of the Chinese authorities, and, following each occupation, the civil administration was reorganized. . . . This . . . cannot be considered as a spontaneous and genuine independence movement.[8]

China accepted the Assembly's report. Japan rejected it, made a statement of its position, and gave notice of intention to withdraw from the League.

The statement of recommendations in the report adopted by the Assembly was presented in three sections.[9] The first section explained that the settlement of the dispute should observe the provisions of the Covenant of the League, the Pact of Paris,

[8] Same, 719.   [9] Same, 721-26.

the Nine-Power Treaty, and the Assembly resolution of March 11, 1932. It was then stated that settlement of the dispute must conform to the following principles and conditions laid down by the Commission of Enquiry: compatibility with the interests of both China and Japan; consideration for the interests of the U.S.S.R.; conformity with existing multilateral treaties; recognition of Japan's interest in Manchuria; the establishment of new treaty relations between China and Japan; effective provision for the settlement of future disputes; Manchurian autonomy; internal order and security against external aggression; encouragement of an economic *rapprochement* between China and Japan; and international co-operation in Chinese reconstruction. The second section recommended the evacuation of Japanese troops present outside the South Manchuria Railway zone; the establishment in Manchuria of an organization under the sovereignty of and compatible with the administrative integrity of China, but with a wide measure of autonomy; and the settlement of questions affecting the "good understanding" between China and Japan by negotiations between the two parties with the assistance of an advisory committee set up by the Assembly.

The third section of the statement of recommendations adopted by the Assembly reaffirmed the application of the doctrine of nonrecognition. "The Members of the League intend to abstain, particularly as regards the existing regime in Manchuria, from any act which might prejudice or delay the carrying out of the recommendations of the said report. They will continue not to recognize this regime either *de jure* or *de facto*. They intend to abstain from taking any isolated action with regard to the situation in Manchuria and to continue to concert their action among themselves as well as with the interested states not members of the League."[10]

After the Sino-Japanese conflict broke out anew in the summer of 1937, the Assembly adopted a resolution, on October 6,

[10] Same, 726. An advisory committee was set up to concert the action of member and nonmember states. The United States accepted the invitation to co-operate with this committee; the U.S.S.R. declined.

providing that the Assembly "solemnly condemns" the aerial bombardment of open towns in China and "expresses its moral support for China, and recommends that Members of the League should refrain from taking any action which might have the effect of weakening China's power of resistance and thus of increasing her difficulties in the present conflict, and should also consider how far they can individually extend aid to China."[11]

On November 3 the parties to the Nine-Power Treaty convened at Brussels to discuss the Sino-Japanese conflict. Japan refused repeated invitations to be present at this conference, and on November 15 a declaration was adopted asserting, in part, that the conflict was a matter of concern to all nations, that there was no warrant in law for the use of armed forces for intervention in the internal regime of another country, and that a just and lasting settlement could not be achieved by direct negotiations between China and Japan. The declaration concluded: "Though hoping that Japan will not adhere to her refusal the States represented at Brussels must consider what is to be their common attitude in a situation where one party to an international treaty maintains against the views of all the other parties that the action which it has taken does not come within the scope of that treaty, and sets aside provisions of the treaty which the other parties hold to be operative in the circumstances."[12]

Again no definite action was taken against Japan, and a few weeks later the conference was indefinitely adjourned, after adopting on November 24 another declaration expressing concern in the conflict, reaffirming the principles of the Nine-Power Treaty, and urging that hostilities be suspended.[13] The same attitude was reaffirmed by the Council of the League in May and again in September, 1938.[14]

[11] League of Nations, *Official Journal*, Special Supplement No. 169, pp. 120-25, 148-49.
[12] United States Department of State, *Press Releases*, November 20, 1937, pp. 380-82.
[13] Same, November 27, 1937, pp. 399-401.
[14] League of Nations, *Official Journal*, 1938, pp. 378, 878-80.

From this summary it will be seen that the attitude and policies of the League of Nations toward the Sino-Japanese dispute were based on a collective concern in the existence and settlement of international conflict. Japanese action was considered to be in violation of the Covenant of the League, the Pact of Paris, and the Nine-Power Treaty. Measures based upon this judgment consisted of attempts at conciliation and mediation, use of the technique of inquiry, and finally, application of the doctrine of nonrecognition. Conciliation, mediation, and inquiry were pre-World War I techniques, but in connection with the Sino-Japanese conflict their scope was somewhat extended in that they were used in concert by a large number of third states applying a common concern and attitude, rather than as the isolated efforts of a small number of third states acting individually. Furthermore, it was no longer considered that one party to the dispute could unilaterally reject tenders of conciliation and inquiry, retaining its freedom to judge the rightfulness of its own action so far as international law and organization were concerned. Methods of pacific settlement designed to restrict the scope and frequency of international violence when each state was the recognized ultimate judge of the legitimacy of its own participation in war remained useful for attempts to restrict international violence after acceptance of the principle of concern had provided the basis for third-party judgment on the validity of participation in war. But the context, and therefore the functional significance, of these traditional methods had changed. The implications of their rejection by one of the parties were different. What had formerly been the main reliance of peace efforts had become the first mild steps in the collective search for a peaceful solution. Their failure now meant not a recovery of freedom of action by the disputants, but the occasion for the consideration of collective measures of greater efficacy.

The doctrine of nonrecogntion went farther. It was applied for the first time as a collective sanction against one party to an international conflict. Neither the traditional methods nor the innovation was adequate to achieve their purpose in the

Sino-Japanese conflict. The League did not see fit to declare that Japan had "resorted to war" in violation of the Covenant, Article 16 was not invoked, and economic and military sanctions were not applied.[15] It took more than nonrecognition and appeals to public opinion to get the Japanese army out of China. This case of international conflict persisted and spread; it was not brought under control by group action based on the principle of concern.

(b) *The Chaco Dispute*

Claims to the territory known as El Gran Chaco had been a source of controversy between Bolivia and Paraguay for more than a century. An outbreak of hostilities in December, 1928, brought the conflict to the attention of the League Council and the International Conference of American States meeting at Washington.[16] The 1928 incidents were settled in September, 1929, by a Commission of Neutrals set up by the Conference of American States, but the basic territorial dispute was not resolved. Hostilities broke out once more in 1932. The Commission of Neutrals made efforts at mediation, and in August, 1932, the nineteen American republics (other than the parties) directed a common appeal to both Bolivia and Paraguay, including a warning that they would not "recognize any territorial arrangement which has not been obtained by peaceful means nor the validity of territorial acquisitions which may be obtained through occupation or conquest by force of arms."[17]

The dispute continued, and the four states bordering on the disputants—Argentina, Brazil, Chile, and Peru—showed an increasing tendency to intervene. The Argentine Foreign Office

[15] Great Britain did declare an embargo on certain shipments of arms to the Far East on February 26, 1933, but lifted it on the following March 13.

[16] For the Chaco dispute, see League of Nations, *Report of the Chaco Commission;* same, *Official Journal,* Special Supplement Nos. 124, 132-135; Russell M. Cooper, *American Consultation in World Affairs,* 109-191; Helen Paull Kirkpatrick, "The League and the Chaco Dispute"; same, "The Chaco Dispute"; Mary Mattison, "The Chaco Arms Embargo."

[17] United States Department of State, *Press Releases,* August 3, 1932.

was especially critical, accusing the Commission of Neutrals of using the Monroe Doctrine to prevent action by the League of Nations, of which both Bolivia and Paraguay were members.[18] The League had not assumed any jurisdiction over the dispute, apparently in part because of a reluctance to interfere with the Commission of Neutrals. However, there was the further fact that neither party to the dispute had invoked its aid. The Council of the League took its first active step in September, 1932, by appointing a Committee of Three to follow the dispute. In December, 1932, the Commission of Neutrals submitted a comprehensive peace proposal, but Paraguay rejected it. A peace plan drafted by the foreign ministers of Argentina and Chile, and presented with the support of Brazil and Peru, likewise was not accepted.

On May 10, 1933, Paraguay issued a declaration of war. The Council of the League then outlined a basis for negotiations, which was rejected by Bolivia. However, both parties agreed to accept an inquiry by the League, and the Commission of Neutrals withdrew in order that negotiations might be centered in Geneva. A League Commission of Enquiry was set up in Montevideo by the first week in November, 1933, and carried on its investigations until the middle of March, 1934. In December, 1933, a truce was declared as a result of the co-operation of the Pan-American Conference then meeting in Montevideo, but the hostilities were resumed in January. The report of the Commission of Enquiry set forth the geographic and historic aspects of the dispute, proposed a settlement, and recommended an embargo on the shipment of arms to both parties. This report was approved by the Council in May, 1934, and by August 1 the recommended embargo had been applied by twenty-eight states. The United States co-operated in this measure.

The report adopted by the Council was, however, not satisfactory to either Bolivia or Paraguay. The former, in an attempt to have Paraguay declared the aggressor and sanctions applied, invoked Article 12 and then Article 15 of the Cove-

[18] See Kirkpatrick, "The League and the Chaco Dispute," 111.

nant, and asked to have the dispute referred to the Assembly. Paraguay, for its part, made a number of observations on the report and in effect rejected it, alleging among other things that it was partial to the Bolivian viewpoint. Further efforts of other American states to settle the dispute during the summer of 1934 proved futile.

The Assembly of the League at its meeting in September referred the question to its Sixth (Political) Committee. Paraguay objected to the application of Article 15, claiming that it did not cover a case where war had already broken out and conciliation had been attempted. That government preferred conciliation under Article 11 and recourse to the Permanent Court. Paraguay argued that the words "likely to lead to a rupture" could not apply when the rupture had already occurred and had led to war. The question of the correctness of this contention was referred to the First (Legal) Committee, which decided that the words quoted were meant to exclude minor and unimportant disputes. Otherwise, a member of the League could evade the application of sanctions against itself merely by issuing a declaration of war. The Assembly then proceeded to discuss the arms embargo, particularly the question of whether it should be applied to both parties rather than only to the one designated as an aggressor.

As a result of its deliberations the Assembly adopted on September 27, 1934, a resolution calling for conciliation under Article 15, paragraph 3. This task was entrusted to a Conciliation Committee composed of the members of the Council and certain other states. If conciliation failed, the committee was to draw up a report containing a statement of the facts, recommendations for settlement, and any further measures for arms prohibition that might be necessary. Both parties persisted in their hostile attitudes, and the committee had to abandon its negotiations looking to a settlement. In November it drew up the report contemplated in the circumstances by its instructions. This report was adopted by the Assembly in an extraordinary session on November 20, 1934. Both Bolivia and Paraguay were severely criticized for failure to appeal to the League immediately upon the outbreak of war. The recommendations proposed the cessation of hostilities and settlement of the substantive question. A detailed procedure was outlined for withdrawal of both armies under international supervision, for the taking of measures to insure the maintenance of peace, for the final delimitation of the frontier, and for arriving at the economic clauses of the treaty of peace. With reference to the arms embargo the report adopted by the Assembly included the following resolution: "The Assembly, having regard to the exceptional circumstances of the present case, and without in any way creating a precedent, approves, as one of the measures to obtain and maintain cessation of hostilities, the prohibition of supply of arms and war material to Bolivia and Paraguay, and it recommends to the members of the League of Nations in the subsequent decisions which they may have to take as regards the maintenance, possible modification or withdrawal of such prohibition, to have regard to the action taken by each of the Parties upon the Assembly's recommendations."[19]

This report and proposed settlement was accepted by Bolivia but rejected by Paraguay.[20] The Advisory Committee which had been constituted by the Assembly to assist in co-ordinating the action of the various governments recommended on January 16, 1935, that the embargo on arms shipments to Bolivia be lifted. No mention was made of Article 16, but there was an implication that Paraguay should be considered the aggressor. Otherwise, why a recommendation of adverse differential treatment for that country? During February eleven states, including some of the principal arms manufacturing countries, lifted the arms embargo against Bolivia. However, the United States maintained the dual embargo, and no Latin American member of the League raised the embargo against Bolivia. The discriminatory embargo failed to settle the dispute, just as the impartial one had. One result, however, was that Paraguay gave notice of its withdrawal from the League, as Japan had done two years before.

[19] League of Nations, *Official Journal,* Special Supplement No. 132, p. 51.
[20] The Paraguayan army was overwhelmingly victorious at this particular time.

The questions of the legal consequences of Paraguay's withdrawal and of the possibility of invoking Article 16 were raised when the Advisory Committee met on March 11, 1935. It was evident that further sanctions could be applied only after a determination that there had been a resort to war within the meaning of Article 16. Three different proposals were submitted. The first, suggested by the U.S.S.R., favored immediate application of sanctions against Paraguay for rejection of the Assembly's recommendation. The second, urged by Italy, proposed that the question be referred to the Permanent Court, since sanctions could not be applied until there was an identification of the original aggressor. The third proposal, favored by France, suggested that the South American states recommend the next steps to be taken. Determining the aggressor was a difficult problem. Neither party had submitted the dispute in its earlier stages to the League, and this constituted a violation of the Covenant. When the League assumed jurisdiction, war had already broken out. Assuming that a clear determination of the original fault could be made, two alternatives would be possible. If Paraguay were held responsible, the original aggressor and the party rejecting the Assembly's recommendations would be one and the same. No great difficulty would seem to arise in reaching a definitive conclusion about the proper object of sanctions. However, if Bolivia were held to be the original aggressor, the question would arise whether a violator of the Covenant could remove the stigma of aggression by subsequent compliance with the League's recommendations for the settlement of a conflict for whose origin it was responsible.

As a matter of fact, it was decided to leave the decision to an extraordinary session of the Assembly, convoked for May 20. However, an American group of mediators had been set up a few weeks earlier, and on May 18 the two belligerents accepted the principle of direct negotiations. The Assembly, meeting two days later, was therefore able to take note of this progress, to express its hope that successful results would be achieved, and to authorize the Advisory Committee to follow the negotiations and report to the Assembly in September. During the summer hostilities ceased,[21] and a peace conference opened at Buenos Aires on July 1, 1935. Demobilization and the restoration of the war area to its previous civilian uses proceeded with little difficulty, but settlement of the issues in controversy was not achieved even after several months of negotiations. However, on October 28 the peace conference announced that although no settlement of the war guilt and territorial questions had been reached, the war itself had come to an end.

The Chaco dispute presented a difficult and complicated situation. The efforts to settle it were many, long, and tedious. The cessation of hostilities was finally achieved, but certainly that circumstance was by no means a brilliant or clear-cut victory for the processes of peaceful settlement. However, the above sketch of the main points in the attempts at settlement reveals the expression of a collective concern in the existence of international conflict, an application of the doctrine of non-recognition, and a discrimination through an arms embargo of the party rejecting the recommendations made by the Assembly of the League. Measures based upon the principle of concern were utilized to an extent, and it seems reasonable to conclude that the resulting collective pressure had something to do with restraining the scope and duration of this particular incident of international conflict.

(c) *The Italo-Ethiopian War*

The relation of the collective attitude in the Italo-Ethiopian War to the principle of concern can be stated simply. That principle was used, but partially and ineffectively. Italy was the first member of the League[22] ever to be found guilty of a "resort to war" in violation of the Covenant, and the attack on

---

[21] By this time Paraguay had met with reverses and the war had developed into a wearisome stalemate for both sides.

[22] And the only one, except for the expulsion of the Soviet Union for the attack on Finland in 1939 after World War II had already started.

Ethiopia was the only incident in which the sanctions of Article 16 were invoked.

Several futile attempts were made by the League to find a solution for the dispute which led to the Italo-Ethiopian War of 1935-1936, but the Italian government persisted in rejecting all efforts for a peaceful settlement.[23] On October 3, 1935, Italian military airplanes bombarded Adowa and Adigrat, and a battle took place in the province of Agame. These events were characterized by Italy as "necessary measures of defense" resulting from the Ethiopian general mobilization of September 28 and the "continual and sanguinary aggression to which Italy has been subjected in the last ten years." The Ethiopian government claimed that these facts occurring in Ethiopian territory involved a violation of the frontiers of the empire and a breach of the Covenant by Italian aggression.

The League was thus confronted with the necessity for some decision and some action. Alternative major conclusions may be drawn from this affair. The first is that the sanctions of Article 16, based as they were on the principle of concern, were applied and that the application was ineffective. The second is that the application of sanctions was based less on acceptance of the principle of concern than on the limitation by interpretation which had occurred early in the history of the League.[24]

The finding of the Council committee set up to make a report on the affair was that "the Italian Government has resorted to war in disregard of its covenants under Article XII of the Covenant of the League of Nations." On October 7, 1935, the states represented upon the Council accepted this verdict, "recording their opinions individually; thus each State decided for itself on the evidence that resort to war had taken place

[23] For accounts of the Italo-Ethiopian War and the application of sanctions, see League of Nations, *Official Journal*, 1935, pp. 639-43, 720-59; same, Special Supplement Nos. 138, 145-151; Royal Institute of International Affairs, *Documents on International Affairs, 1935*, II; same, *International Sanctions*; Rappard, *The Quest for Peace*, 188-205, 279-317; Quincy Wright, "The Test of Aggression in the Italo-Ethiopian War," *American Journal of International Law*, XXX (1936), 27-44; Walters, *A History of the League of Nations*, II, 623-91.

[24] See Chapter III, section 2.

in disregard of obligations under Article 12, and having so decided recognized that the specific case for the application of the measures prescribed in Article 16 had arisen."

The Assembly was convened on October 9, and the next day the same conclusions were accepted (silence being construed as acceptance) by all the member states except Italy, Austria, Hungary, and Albania. In the voting, the individual assent of each government was required.

A Co-ordination Committee consisting of all members of the Assembly except the belligerent states was appointed to make recommendations upon the detailed application of sanctions. During October the Co-ordination Committee recommended that the arms embargo which certain states had applied against Italy and Ethiopia be raised from the latter and that there be applied against Italy an arms embargo, a credit embargo, an import boycott, an export embargo on certain key products, and a provision for mutual support in the application of economic and financial measures. The committee then adjourned and left a Subcommittee of Eighteen to continue the co-ordination of sanctions, which went into effect on November 18.

The interpretative principle that sanctions may be applied gradually and partially was followed. The application of sanctions was delayed, and many key products were omitted from the embargo list. Under the circumstances oil was the most important material to be excluded. The extension of the export embargo to oil and other strategic products was discussed, but no action was taken. The "peculiar position" of various states was also a factor in the application of sanctions against Italy. The proposals of the Co-ordination Committee were accepted by all the states members of the League except Albania, Austria, Ecuador, Hungary, and Paraguay. (Guatemala, Honduras, and Salvador accepted "in principle.")[25]

[25] Albania declined to take action, in view of her alliance with Italy. Paraguay took no part, as her notice of withdrawal from the League had been given on February 24, 1935. The German government took measures to control abnormal trading operations. No action was taken by Japan and Brazil. Egypt was the only nonmember of the League to participate in the application of sanctions. The United States on October 3 recognized a state of war as existing and applied an arms embargo against both belligerents.

The representative of Austria stated in the Assembly on October 9: "Loyalty towards the League makes it incumbent upon my Government at once to draw your attention to the serious dangers which sanctions will inevitably entail in the economic life of Europe, in particular for those smaller States whose capacity for economic and financial resistance has been considerably reduced by the unfavourable conditions imposed upon them. My Government is not thinking only of Austria, but also of its creditors."[26]

On the same occasion the Hungarian representative said:

As regards economic sanctions, Hungary is in a very special position. In numerous reports and resolutions of the League of Nations concerning Article 16 of the Covenant, it has been laid down that account must be taken of the special conditions and requirements of certain countries and that certain forms of economic action might produce very harmful effects on the very countries which adopt them and might, indeed, involve these countries in serious danger. Consequently, I think that it would be more in keeping with the League's aims to allow Members of the League some degree of latitude. Nobody can be better aware than the Council, which has for years been supervising the finances of Hungary, of the economic and financial difficulties experienced by my country. The exclusion of Italy from Hungary's restricted and limited trade outlets would completely upset our economic and financial equilibrium, which has hitherto been preserved at great cost, largely by means of export to Italy.[27]

Switzerland made certain reservations and on October 12 regretted her inability to enforce the import embargo because of her Italian population. The statement of its representative is of particular interest. He said:

The status of the Swiss Confederation, in so far as its external relations are concerned, continues to be governed by the principle of neutrality. This is the outcome of the history, traditions, written constitution, and racial composition of the country. Our neutrality

[26] League of Nations, *Official Journal*, Special Supplement No. 138, 1935, p. 101; Royal Institute of International Affairs, *Documents on International Affairs, 1935*, II, 185-86.
[27] League of Nations, *Official Journal*, Special Supplement No. 138, 1935, p. 101; Royal Institute of International Affairs, *Documents on International Affairs, 1935*, II, 187.

is incorporated in international law; it has been recognized as being in conformity with the interest, firstly, of Europe, and secondly of the entire world; the declaration made in London by the Council of the League of Nations on February 13, 1920, confirmed it in solemn terms. The Confederation would not have agreed to enter the League if the price of its participation had been the abandonment of its ancient status. Everything that we have seen, observed, and experienced at Geneva since 1920 has confirmed us in the conviction that our attitude was a wise one.

Consequently, our general obligations to take part in economic and financial sanctions to the exclusion of any military sanctions, is not absolute, but must be interpreted in the light of the resolution of 1921 regarding the economic weapon. The limits of our obligation are determined by our neutrality, which, in our opinion, constitutes a fundamental principle and at the same time a vital interest. We do not feel ourselves bound to take part in sanctions which, by their nature and effect, would expose our neutrality to real dangers—dangers which we must judge in the full exercise of our sovereignty.[28]

The modification of the application of sanctions by taking account of the "peculiar position" of the member states was, however, by no means confined to the governments making the formal declarations quoted above. France, for example, found that the price of carrying out the obligations of Article 16 would be the alienation of a possible ally against Germany. As one observer saw it, the French hoped "that they might be able to sabotage the application of the Covenant against Italy in order to preserve this self-same Covenant intact for future use against Germany—with a triumphant Italian Covenant-breaker helping France, in the name of the Covenant, to hold Germany in check!"[29]

Thus, in the only effort of the League to apply sanctions under Article 16, each state decided for itself whether an occasion for the invocation of sanctions had arisen, the coercive measures were applied gradually and partially, and the "pe-

[28] League of Nations, *Official Journal*, Special Supplement No. 138, 1935, pp. 106, 107; Royal Institute of International Affairs, *Documents on International Affairs, 1935*, II, 189, 190.

[29] Arnold J. Toynbee, *Survey of International Affairs, 1935*, II, 4. It is, of course, obvious that the fundamental axiom of diplomacy is concern for the "peculiar position" of one's state.

culiar positions" of the member states had to be taken into consideration. In fact, the application of sanctions was gradual and partial to the extent that the apparent obligation of immediate and complete severance of economic relations was interpreted and limited so that only those supplies not vitally needed by the aggressor were withheld. As Rappard wrote, "The sanctions finally agreed to and applied were extremely mild. They in fact merely tended to hamper Italy's foreign trade, to limit her imports of war materials, not including oil, and to weigh on her balance of payments."[30]

Little need be said of the outcome of this one case of the application of sanctions. Italy proceeded to conquer Ethiopia and to present the League with a embarrassing *fait accompli*. The failure of sanctions was officially recognized by the Assembly on July 4, 1936. The discussions of the preceding few days centered around the theme of recognizing the inevitable. Finally, a vote was taken on a resolution declaring faithful adherence to Articles 10 and 16 of the Covenant, affirming the doctrine of nonrecognition, and recommending assistance to Ethiopia. This resolution was lost by a majority of 23 to 1, with 25 governments abstaining.[31]

Sanctions as applied did not restrain Italy, save Ethiopia, or implement collective security. As a matter of fact, half-hearted and ineffective sanctions were probably worse than none. The following paragraph is worth pondering not only in connection with the Italo-Ethiopian War, but also because it provides an illustration of one kind of pitfall to be avoided in attempts at the control of international conflict:

As it turned out . . . the action of the League was not only negative as far as stopping Italy was concerned. It was actually of positive assistance to her rulers. One of the jokes current in Rome after the war was over was a saying that the Italian Empire had been founded by Cavour, Mussolini, and the League of Nations. To the Fascist Government, in fact, sanctions were a godsend. Up to that moment the country was far from being united by the

[30] *The Quest for Peace*, 298.
[31] League of Nations, *Records of the Sixteenth Assembly*, Plenary Meetings, 68.

adventure. During the preparatory period, as Marshal De Bono himself admits, there were constant grumblings on the home front. Defeatism was rampant and was encouraged by reports of disorganization in the colonies. Many Italians were saying openly that the enterprise was too difficult and would lead them to ruin. There were rumours of disaffection between the Army and the Fascist Party and even of a rift between the King and Mussolini. But as soon as it became clear that Italy was to be penalized all opposition was silenced. A common indignation welded the nation together.[32]

2. Policy of the United States

Without ever becoming a member, the United States played an important role in the development of the League system. We have seen that the United States took a leading part in securing acceptance of the principle of concern after World War I, in limiting that acceptance by its rejection of the Covenant, and in working out a modified application especially in connection with the Pact of Paris and the Stimson Doctrine. It is therefore appropriate to inquire whether the United States took any comparable leading part in the fourth and last phase of the principle of concern during the period 1933-1939. In connection with such an inquiry, the question arises of the relation of the policy and attitude of the United States to the major incidents of international conflict handled by the League of Nations.

Before considering the relation of the United States toward the League's position with respect to three major incidents of international conflict, it is important to note that the principle of concern was accepted to some extent by the United States government. That was basic to the Pact of Paris and the Stimson Doctrine. The Roosevelt administration continued this tradition. The idea that international conflict anywhere is the

[32] George Martelli, *Italy Against the World*, 163. Rappard reached the same conclusion, saying, "As it was, the action of the League, sufficiently unfriendly to arouse the national pride of the Fascist Kingdom, yet insufficiently drastic and determined to deter her daring but realistic leader from the undertaking on which he had set his heart, hastened rather than impeded the conquest of Ethiopia." *The Quest for Peace*, 298.

concern of all nations was stated on a number of occasions by the President and the Secretary of State, and Roosevelt's famous "quarantine" speech of October 5, 1937, contained the statement: "The peace-loving nations must make a concerted effort in opposition to those violations of treaties and those ignorings of humane instincts which today are creating a state of international anarchy and instability from which there is no escape through mere isolation or neutrality. . . . International anarchy destroys every foundation for peace. It jeopardizes either the immediate or the future security of every nation, large or small."[33]

The position of the United States with respect to the Sino-Japanese and Chaco disputes will now be summarized briefly, and some of the problems raised by the application of sanctions against Italy will be indicated.

It will be recalled that the United States took the lead in applying the doctrine of nonrecognition against the Japanese conquest of Manchuria. When hostilities again broke out in the summer of 1937, the question of application of the Neutrality Act of 1935 became relevant. During the Italo-Ethiopian controversy the President accepted "the engaging of armed forces in combat" as the test of the existence of war. This was certainly happening in China; yet the Neutrality Act was not invoked. This time the definition of war posited certain formalities in addition to actual "armed invasion and a resultant killing of human beings." In a statement of policy with respect to the Sino-Japanese controversy Secretary Hull said on August 23 that "from the beginning of the present controversy in the Far East, we have been urging upon the Chinese and the Japanese Governments the importance of refraining from hostilities and of maintaining peace. We have been participating constantly in consultation with interested governments directed toward peaceful adjustment. This Government does not believe in political alliances or entanglements, nor does it believe in extreme isolation."[34]

[33] United States Department of State, *Press Releases,* October 9, 1937.
[34] Same, August 28, 1937.

On September 14 the President issued a statement prohibiting merchant vessels owned by the United States government from transporting arms, ammunition, and implements of war to China or Japan, and giving notice that any privately owned American merchant vessels would transport such cargoes at their own risk. The President's statement added, "The question of applying the Neutrality Act remains *in statu quo*, the Government policy remaining on a twenty-four hour basis."[35]

On October 5, 1937, President Roosevelt made his famous "quarantine" speech in Chicago, one of the purposes of which was to test public reaction toward some sort of collecive action to restrain aggression. He said in that speech: "We are determined to keep out of war, yet we cannot insure ourselves against the disastrous effects of war and the dangers of involvement. We are adopting such measures as will minimize our risk of involvement, but we cannot have complete protection in a world of disorder in which confidence and security have broken down."[36]

In reference to the resolution adopted by the Assembly of the League on October 6, the United States government asserted that the action of Japan in China was contrary to the Nine-Power Treaty and the Pact of Paris, and that "the conclusions of this Government . . . are in general accord with those of the Assembly of the League of Nations."[37] The United States took a leading part in convening the Nine-Power Conference which met at Brussels on November 3. The conference produced nothing practical, however, and the policy of the United States toward the Sino-Japanese conflict remained *"in statu quo"*—hostilities were continued, no collective action was taken to stop the conflict, and the Neutrality Act was not applied.

If the Sino-Japanese conflict was an instance of co-operation with the League by the United States, the Chaco dispute was one of parallel action in applying an arms embargo against both parties, but not in subsequently lifting it to discriminate

[35] Same, September 18, 1937.   [36] Same, October 9, 1937, p. 279.
[37] Same, October 9, 1937.

against Paraguay. The 1934 session of Congress enacted no arms embargo legislation which contemplated modification of the neutrality policy of the United States or which was passed primarily as a means of safeguarding American neutrality. However, Congress did authorize the President to prohibit the sale of arms and munitions of war in the United States to the Chaco belligerents.

Congressional action in this matter coincided with an attempt by the League of Nations to secure a general arms embargo against Bolivia and Paraguay. At the Council meeting of May 17, 1934, while the report of the Chaco Commission of Enquiry was under discussion, the British government raised the question of an arms embargo as a contribution to bringing hostilities to an end.[38] Two days later the Council adopted a resolution requesting a Committee of Three to proceed with the necessary consultations. On May 20 a telegram was sent to the United States Secretary of State seeking information about whether his government was prepared to participate with other governments in prohibiting the sale of arms and munitions of war to Bolivia and Paraguay. On May 22 Secretary Hull recommended favorable action on resolutions which had recently been introduced into Congress and which were designed to prohibit the sale of arms to the two countries. The House resolution was passed the next day; the Senate concurred on May 24; the President gave his approval on May 28 and issued a proclamation putting the act into effect.[39]

The Bolivian government immediately protested against such action by the United States, alleging in a note of June 1 that the prohibition was in violation of a treaty of 1858 in effect between the United States and Bolivia, which provided, "nor shall any prohibition be imposed on the importation or exportation of any articles, the produce or manufactures of the Republic of Bolivia or of the United States, which shall not equally extend to all other nations." It was further contended

[38] League of Nations, *Official Journal*, 1934, pp. 754-56.
[39] United States Congress, *Congressional Record*, 73d Cong., 2d Sess., 9375, 9428, 9430, 9432-34; United States Department of State, *Press Releases*, June 2, 1934.

that the prohibition was unfair to Bolivia because Paraguay enjoyed access to an international waterway.[40] Secretary Hull in a note of June 13 answered these contentions by pointing out, first, that the treaty of 1858 related to importation and exportation while the resolution prohibited only the sale of arms and munitions of war in the United States to the Chaco belligerents, and second, that the international waterway was of no advantage to Paraguay because that country was prohibited from obtaining by any means of transportation arms and munitions of war sold in the United States.

The prohibition on the sale of arms and munitions in the United States remained applicable to both parties until it was revoked by a proclamation of November 14, 1935, effective from November 29, after the peace conference at Buenos Aires had adopted on October 28, 1935, a resolution declaring that the war between Bolivia and Paraguay had come to an end.

Upon the outbreak of the Italo-Ethiopian War the immediate question for the United States was whether the provisions of the Neutrality Act of 1935 were applicable to the conflict. Neither country had declared war; yet hostilities were being conducted on a rather extensive scale. Whether or not an embargo should be declared by the United States government depended on whether or not war had "broken out" or was "in progress." President Roosevelt adopted as a test of the existence of war the engaging of armed forces in combat. In a statement made at the time he issued an embargo proclamation on October 5, he said, "we are now compelled to recognize the simple and indisputable fact that Ethiopian and Italian armed forces are engaged in combat, thus creating a state of war within the intent and meaning of the joint resolution."[41] In his Armistice Day address a little more than a month later the President said, "We are acting to simplify definitions and facts by calling war 'war' when armed invasion and a resulting killing of human beings takes place."[42]

Definition of the Italo-Ethiopian conflict as war was in

[40] United States Department of State, *Press Releases*, June 16, 1934.
[41] Same, October 5, 1935.   [42] Same, November 16, 1935.

advance of such action by other nations. The members of the Council of the League agreed on October 7 that Italy had "resorted to war" in violation of its obligations under Article 12 of the Covenant, and this position was immediately accepted by the states represented in the Assembly.[43] Such a situation might raise the interesting question of whether the juridical position of the United States was, for a few days, different from that of other states. Would Italy and Ethiopia have belligerent rights and duties with respect to the United States, but not toward any other nation? Perhaps it could be argued that war within the meaning of the joint resolution was not necessarily war in the international sense.

The declaration of an arms embargo also raised the question of a definition of arms, ammunition, and implements of war, since the joint resolution passed by Congress provided that "the President, by proclamation, shall definitely enumerate the arms, ammunition, or implements of war, the export of which is prohibited by this Act." There was some question of whether all supplies essential to the conduct of war could by definition be included in such a category. However, it was interpreted by the President as including only those "munitions of war" used in actual combat between armed forces. This interpretation was in accordance with the clear intent of Congress. A specific grant of power to impose an embargo on all supplies used in war had not been included in the joint resolution, and on the Senate floor it had been understood that the more restricted interpretation was to be given to this particular part of the act.[44] The list of articles to be considered arms, ammunition, or implements of war was included in the President's embargo proclamation. The list was identical with that adopted, on recommendation of the National Munitions Control Board, by a proclamation of September 25 for the administration of section two of the act. It included substantially the same articles as the Geneva Arms Trade Convention, the most

[43] Royal Institute of International Affairs, *Documents on International Affairs, 1935*, II, 183-91.
[44] United States Congress, *Congressional Record*, 74th Cong., 1st Sess., 13954.

important difference being that certain gases named in the President's proclamation were not in the Geneva agreement.

When the embargo proclamation was issued, it also became unlawful, under Section 3 of the joint resolution, for any American vessel "to carry any arms, ammunition, or implements of war to any port of the belligerent countries . . . or to any neutral port for transshipment to, or for the use of, a belligerent country." On the same day (October 5) the President issued a second proclamation giving notice that any citizen of the United States who might travel on a vessel of either of the belligerents contrary to the provisions of the joint resolution would do so at his own risk. There was no occasion to place restrictions on the use of American ports by submarines or as a base of supply for belligerent warships.

The policy of the United States government toward the Italo-Ethiopian conflict, as announced by the President, went further than was required by the act of Congress. In his statement which accompanied the embargo proclamation President Roosevelt, after referring to the "state of war" between Ethiopian and Italian armed forces, said, "In these specific circumstances I desire it to be understood that any of our people who voluntarily engage in transactions of any character with either of the belligerents do so at their own risk."[45]

The determination that the United States should not become involved in a foreign war, rather than the purpose to protect the full legal rights of every citizen, was presented as the fundamental policy of the Roosevelt administration. The President in his speech of October 2, 1935, at San Diego said, "We not only earnestly desire peace, but we are moved by a stern determination to avoid those perils that will endanger our peace with the world."[46]

The Secretary of State, when asked in a press conference of October 10 to elaborate on the policy of "transactions at risk," replied: "The warning given by the President in his proclamation concerning travel on belligerent ships and his general

[45] United States Department of State, *Press Releases*, October 5, 1935.
[46] Same, October 12, 1935.

warning that during the war any of our people who voluntarily engage in transactions of any character with either of the belligerents do so at their own risk were based upon the policy and purpose of keeping this country out of war—keeping it from being drawn into war. It certainly was not intended to encourage transactions with the belligerents."[46] In a radio address of October 15, 1935, to the New York *Herald Tribune* Forum on Current Affairs he said that "we are determined not to enter into armed conflicts that may arise between other countries, and to enforce such policies as may be required to avoid that risk. On these matters the great majority of the American people are agreed."[47]

The President, while at sea on the U.S.S. *Houston,* sent a message which was read by Mrs. Roosevelt on October 17 to the Fifth Annual Women's Conference on Current Problems. After referring to the vital interest of women in the preservation of peace, the message continued with the statement that "I have pledged myself to do my part in keeping America free of those entanglements that move us along the road to war."[47]

But all interest in the Italo-Ethiopian conflict and its possible complications could not be renounced. Expressed devotion to the ideal of world peace could not be reconciled with indifference to the possibility of unnecessarily prolonging a war anywhere in the world. The official position on this point was well summarized in an address of the Secretary of State on "Our Foreign Policy with Respect to Neutrality," written for delivery over the radio on the evening of November 6, 1935. The address concluded with the following words:

Moreover, we should not concentrate entirely on means for remaining neutral and lose sight of other constructive methods of avoiding involvement in wars between other countries. Our foreign policy would indeed be a weak one if it began or ended with the announcement of a neutral position on the outbreak of a foreign war. I conceive it to be our duty and in the interest of our country and of humanity, not only to remain aloof from disputes and con-

[47] Same, October 19, 1935.

flicts with which we have no direct concern, but also to use our influence in any appropriate way to bring about the peaceful settlement of international differences. Our own interest and our duty as a great power forbid that we shall sit idly by and watch the development of hostilities with a feeling of self-sufficiency and complacency when by the use of our influence, short of becoming involved in the dispute itself, we might prevent or lessen the scourge of war. In short, our policy as a member of the community of nations should be twofold: first, to avoid being brought into a war, and second, to promote as far as possible the interests of international peace and good will. A virile policy tempered with prudent caution is necessary if we are to retain the respect of other nations and at the same time hold our position of influence for peace and international stability in the family of nations.

In summary, while our primary aim should be to avoid involvement in other people's difficulties and hence to lessen our chances of being drawn into a war, we should, on appropriate occasions and within reasonable bounds, use our influence toward the prevention of war and the miseries that attend and follow in its wake. For after all, if peace obtains, problems regarding neutrality will not arise.[48]

Did the United States exert any effective influence for peace in the Italo-Ethiopian conflict?

The Emperor of Ethiopia had chosen the anniversary of American independence as a dramatic time at which to ask the American government to examine means of securing observance of the Pact of Paris. The answer of the United States expressed gratification that the League of Nations was giving its attention to the controversy and that arbitration was in progress. The Ethiopian appeal to the Pact of Paris received no answer beyond the statement that the United States government "would be loath to believe that either of them [Italy and Ethiopia] would resort to other than pacific means as a method of dealing with this controversy or would permit any situation to arise which would be inconsistent with the commitments of the Pact."[49]

The neutrality resolution of August 31, 1935, and the proclamations issued under its authorization, whatever their merits

[48] Same, November 9, 1935.   [49] Same, July 6, 1935.

as an American policy, had little power to prevent or discourage the Italo-Ethiopian conflict. According to the best figures available to the State Department the value of exports of war matériel to Italy and Italian colonies from January 1, 1935, to September 23, 1935, was about $340,000 (nearly all of which was accounted for by airplane engines and parts), as compared with no exports of this type to Ethiopia or French Somaliland.[50] An embargo on "arms, ammunition, and implements of war" would have no effect on Ethiopia, which was not getting such articles from the United States anyhow. Italy had munitions factories and was in a position to fabricate her own arms, provided the necessary raw materials were available. The warning to American citizens that they traveled on the vessels of a belligerent at their own risk may have led to some loss to Italian steamship lines, but could hardly be classed as a deterrent to war.

Since the League of Nations was attempting to stop Mussolini's African campaign by the imposition of sanctions, the most important test of the war-prevention influence of American policy must be found in the effects of that policy on the efforts of the League. In this connection two questions must be considered: (1) As no neutrality policy can be completely impartial in effect, were the results of American action more favorable to the nation against which the League was acting or to the other party? (2) Was the American policy a hindrance to the action of the League?[51]

The answer to the first of these questions might seem to be obvious. Since Italy could obtain, and had been obtaining, some arms and the like from the United States, while Ethiopia could not do so, the result of an arms embargo was simply to shut off the supply to Italy. Also, since Ethiopia had no merchant marine, that country could not be adversely affected

---

[50] Same, October 5, 1935.

[51] The answer to the first of these questions is obviously a factor in the answer to the second. The distinction made here is that between the effect of American policy on the two belligerents and the relation of that policy to action of the League relative to the belligerents.

by a warning to American citizens not to travel on the vessels of a belligerent nation. The superficial view that an American policy of impartiality would in effect be adverse to Italy as compared with Ethiopia must be abandoned, however, when it is considered that the heart of the question about which country would be adversely affected lay in the problem of whether an embargo would be imposed on all supplies essential to the conduct of a war. Italy could manufacture arms, but needed American raw materials, such as oil, scrap metal, and cotton. If the United States had included raw materials in its embargo of "munitions of war," the result would have been a serious handicap to Italy. Under the particular circumstances the real incidence of an American embargo depended on what was included in the list of prohibited articles. Restriction of the list of articles used in actual combat was more favorable to Italy than an extension of the list to all articles essential to the conduct of a war. Once it was decided to impose an embargo, the alternatives were a restricted or extended list of embargoed articles. Ethiopia was not able to obtain supplies from the United States in any case, and it was to the interest of Italy for the United States to adopt a restricted list.

At the time, the possibility also had to be taken into consideration that there might be a war between Italy and certain League states, particularly Great Britain. In that case the situation would be quite different. It might seem that refusal of the United States to impose an embargo on all war supplies would give Italy a better chance to defend herself, but if it could be assumed that the navies of Great Britain and her allies would control the seas, Italy would be cut off from American supplies, unless, of course, the United States was prepared to insist with force on its right to trade with Italy. In such conditions the more restricted the list of articles embargoed by the United States the more supplies the enemies of Italy could get from this country. Thus, exactly the same impartial neutrality policy would have entirely different implications for a given belligerent, merely by reason of the addition of another party to the conflict.

The relation between League policy and American policy raised a serious problem. This was especially true because the very materials most essential to Italy, such as oil and cotton, were precisely the ones which it would have been most difficult for the League to control without American co-operation. When the United States Congress did not place an embargo on all war materials or give the President power to do so in co-operation with other nations, the members of the League faced the possibility of cutting off supplies to Italy only to find their trade diverted to American competitors. The United States government was also in a dilemma. If the members of the League placed an embargo on the shipment of essential war materials to Italy, the United States might be left in the position of conflict with the League in its efforts to prevent war. On the other hand, if the United States followed the policies of the League, the Roosevelt administration would lay itself open to the politically damaging charge of attempting to involve the country in "entangling alliances" and "League wars."

In this situation the League restricted its embargoes to articles of which a relatively large part could be controlled by the members of the League, while the Roosevelt administration undertook to discourage shipments of war materials to Italy in excess of normal peacetime trade. Under a recommendation adopted by the Assembly of the League, the Co-ordination Committee on October 21 transmitted to the United States and other nonmembers of the League the recent documents in the Italo-Ethiopian dispute and its own recommendations, with the statement that "the Governments represented on the Coordination Committee would welcome any communication which any non-Member may deem it proper to make . . . or notification of any action which it may be taking in the circumstances."[52]

The purpose of this committee was to ascertain the attitude of the states not members of the League toward the imposition of sanctions against Italy. The reply of the United States gov-

[52] United States Department of State, *Press Releases*, November 2, 1935.

ernment, given on October 26, emphasized devotion to the preservation of peace and called attention to the proclamations of October 5, as well as to the policy of "transactions at risk." There was no direct reference to the League of Nations or to its condemnation of Italy. It was evident that the United States government would pursue an independent policy, but did not wish to sabotage the efforts of the League. The United States would not undertake positive co-operation in the imposition of sanctions, but there would be the passive co-operation of noninterference. The attitude of the United States government as expressed in the reply to the Co-ordination Committee was summarized thus:

Realizing that war adversely affects every country, that it may seriously endanger the economic welfare of each, causes untold human misery, and even threatens the existence of civilization, the United States, in keeping with the letter and spirit of the Pact of Paris and other peace obligations, undertakes at all times not only to exercise its moral influence in favor of peace throughout the world, but to contribute in every practicable way within the limitations of our foreign policy, to that end. It views with sympathetic interest the individual or concerted efforts of other nations to preserve peace or to localize and shorten the duration of war.[52]

President Roosevelt issued a statement on October 30 in which he said that he did not believe the American people would wish "struggles on the battlefield" to be prolonged because of profits to a small number of American citizens and that "accordingly, the American Government is keeping informed as to all shipments consigned for export to both belligerents." On the same day Secretary Hull stated that "the policy of the Government . . . rests primarily upon the recent neutrality act designed to keep the Nation out of war, and upon the further purpose not to aid in protracting the war."[52]

The increase in American exports to Italy led to further official discouragement of such trade. On November 15 Secretary Hull made a statement in which he said that "the American people are entitled to know that there are certain com-

[52] Same.

modities such as oil, copper, trucks, tractors, scrap iron, and scrap steel which are essential war materials, although not actually 'arms, ammunition, or implements of war,' and that according to recent Government trade reports a considerably increased amount of these is being exported for war purposes. This class of trade is directly contrary to the policy of this Government as announced in official statements of the President and Secretary of State, as it is also contrary to the general spirit of the recent neutrality act."[53]

At the time that the Secretary of State made this statement there was considerable discussion concerning the feasibility of the adoption by the League of an oil embargo against Italy. Oil was a commodity of strategic importance in the conflict. If Italy could have no petroleum from other countries, the African campaign would cease when the accumulated supply was exhausted. But it happened that the members of the League, even if they decided for an oil embargo on other grounds, could not control the world supply because of the large quantities produced in the United States. It may have been no accident that Secretary Hull's statement of November 15 placed oil at the top of the list of materials being shipped in increased amounts for war purposes. A week later the Shipping Board Bureau of the Department of Commerce warned the shipping industry, the chief financial backing of which came from the government, that the carrying of essential war materials, such as those mentioned in the statement of the Secretary of State, destined for either of the belligerents was distinctly contrary to the policy of the government.[54]

There were indications that this warning was motivated chiefly by an expectation that the League would impose an oil embargo against Italy and by the desire of the United States government that American citizens would not insist on supplying the petroleum necessary to the Italian war machine. However, the occasion for the United States to come into such a conflict with the League did not arise, as no prohibition was placed on the sale of oil to Italy by League members.

[53] Same, November 16, 1935.   [54] *New York Times*, November 23, 1935.

The question arises whether the American policy of placing an embargo on arms and the like, discouraging the supply of war materials to belligerents, and "viewing with sympathetic interest" the efforts of other nations to preserve peace was effective in accomplishing the purpose of not contributing to the prolongation of war.

It is true that the United States did not interfere with the application of sanctions against Italy by the League, but there is no way to determine to what extent the United States was a factor in the nonapplication of further sanctions. For example, would the League have placed an embargo on oil if there had been no possibility that Italy would be supplied by American producers? There can be no adequate answer to this question until the scholarly world receives the memoirs of the statesmen who made the decision—and probably not even then. It may well be pointed out, however, that the United States was a large producer of oil, that the United States government had announced an "independent policy," and that even if that government should have attempted to curb shipment of oil to Italy, it would have had to rely on extralegal pressure and "moral suasion." The highly complex considerations of European politics may be sufficient to account for the course taken, and the failure to adopt the oil sanction may be attributed to any one or any combination of factors, such as Baldwin's concern for British ships in the Mediterranean, French desire for Italian help against Germany, or a real fear of a general war. It is naive to assume that the action of the League of Nations depended solely upon American policy. At any rate, it seems obvious that the failure to receive the positive co-operation of the United States to that extent reduced the control of the League over supplies to Italy, and Americans must face the fact that abstention from participation in collective action thereby reduces the effectiveness of such collective action.

The situation in which the United States found itself, neither co-operating with the League nor maintaining an attitude of indifference, suggested a combination of *de jure* neutrality with *de facto* discrimination. That is, this government might apply to both sides those measures the incidence of which would be more burdensome for the aggressor than for the victim. For example, if the aggressor but not the victim needed American supplies, a strict embargo could be imposed. However, there is little to recommend a policy of refusing to co-operate in a collective system and at the same time trying not to interfere with it. The effectiveness of collective security depends upon joint, co-ordinated action. The best that a *de facto* "differential neutrality" could achieve would be a negative noninterference. It would be inconsistent with international solidarity and even with any norms at all for the regulation of international violence. No clear and definite policy could be followed, because the situation would change with each war and with each shift in the fortunes of any given war.

3. "DE FACTO REVISION" OF THE COVENANT

The failure of sanctions in the Italo-Ethiopian conflict and the abrogation by Germany of the Locarno system in March, 1936, gave rise to what has been called a *"de facto* revision" of the Covenant. In particular, the small European states could no longer rely on the guarantees of collective security, yet the obligations of Article 16 might make it difficult for them to abstain from war. If the world, and especially Europe, were to be divided into two hostile camps, the smaller states wished to avoid participation on either side. Fearful that the *status quo* powers would employ the machinery of the League to involve them against the nonmember powers, they demanded a tacit or avowed recognition that they were not bound by the coercive obligations of Article 16. They could no longer depend upon the League system for protection; so they wished to avoid the reprisals from powerful and hostile nonmembers which participation in that system might imply.

On July 1, 1936, a joint declaration was signed by the foreign ministers of seven of the smaller European states—Denmark,

Finland, the Netherlands, Norway, Spain, Sweden, and Switzerland. This declaration stated that the foreign ministers had exchanged views "on the effects of current events on the organisation and working of the League of Nations" and that they were in agreement on certain points.[55]

The declaration did not repudiate the League nor state an intention of withdrawing from it, but questioned the force of its obligations, particularly for the seven countries, under the existing circumstances. To quote, "The aggravation of the international situation and the cases of resort to force that have occurred during the last few years, in violation of the Covenant of the League, have given rise in our countries to some doubt whether the conditions in which they undertook the obligations contained in the Covenant still exist to any satisfactory extent."

The foreign ministers did not think that certain parts of the Covenant, especially Article 16, should remain a dead letter while other articles were enforced. They favored the success of the experiment represented by the establishment of the League, but thought it necessary to consider whether the Covenant could be amended, or its application modified, so as to increase the security of states. That their governments would have reservations in the application of sanctions was indicated by the statement of the seven foreign ministers that "we would place it on record that, so long as the Covenant as a whole is applied only incompletely and inconsistently, we are obliged to bear that fact in mind in connection with the application of Article 16."[55]

After a conference of their ministers for foreign affairs on August 20, 1936, the governments of Denmark, Finland, Norway, and Sweden presented to the Secretary-General of the League statements elucidating the position reflected in the Declaration of Seven.[56]

On January 31, 1938, the delegate of Sweden stated before the Special Committee Set Up to Study the Application of the

[55] For the text of the declaration see League of Nations, *Official Journal*, Special Supplement No. 154, 1936, p. 19.
[56] Same, 15-19, 20-23.

Principles of the Covenant that "in practice, the League no longer possesses the characteristics of a coercive League corresponding to the provisions of Article 16 of the Covenant. By the force of events, without any amendment of the Covenant, a practice has become established whereby Members of the League do not consider themselves bound to take coercive action against an aggressor State."[57] In further explaining the official position of the Swedish government, he said, "What is important is that it [the Swedish attitude] should be recognised as a loyal and legitimate interpretation of the fact that changed conditions have made it impossible for the League at the present time to act in conformity with the letter of the provisions of the Covenant." The Swedish delegate continued with the explanation that this was not to imply that the idea of collective security was being abandoned for the future or that the League should renounce the possibility of effectively intervening in a conflict through spontaneous collaboration by its members. Rather, he argued, a frank recognition of weakness was better than maintaining "the fiction of a system of automatic and obligatory sanctions."[58]

The course of Switzerland took the form of an attempt to obtain a renewed recognition of its "unique" position. The Swiss government, after joining in the declaration of July 1, stated in a letter of September 4, 1936, to the Secretary-General that

if, notwithstanding the criticisms it incurs, Article 16 should be retained substantially in its present form, or if the risks it involves should be made still greater, Switzerland would be obliged to call attention once again to her peculiar position, which the Council of the League, in the Declaration of London of February 13th, 1920, described as unique. The Federal Council must in any case point out once more that Switzerland cannot be held to sanctions which, in their nature and through their effects, would seriously endanger her neutrality. That perpetual neutrality is established by age-old tradition, and all Europe joined in recognising its unquestionable advantages over a hundred years ago.[59]

[57] Same, Special Supplement No. 180, 1938, pp. 9-10.
[58] Same, 10.   [59] Same, No. 154, 1936, p. 29.

This position was reiterated in a statement before the Special
Committee of the League on January 31, 1938.[60] The Swiss
representative referred at that time to "a League from which
two great neighbouring Powers have withdrawn and from
which, moreover, two other great Powers in more distant parts
of the world are absent. In our eyes," he continued, "these
facts are decisive. They deprive differential neutrality of its
political and psychological basis. They make the application
of Article 16 by Switzerland impossible."[61]

The claim of Switzerland to a special position was recognized
by the Council of the League on May 14, 1938. The Council,
by a resolution of this date, "takes note that Switzerland, invoking her perpetual neutrality, has expressed the intention
not to participate any longer in any manner in the putting
into operation of the provisions of the Covenant relating to
sanctions and declares that she will not be invited to do so;
And places on record that the Swiss Government declares its
determination to maintain unaltered in all other respects her
position as a Member of the League, and to continue to give
the facilities which have been accorded to the League for the
free exercise by its institutions of their activities in Swiss territory."[62]

The events of 1935-1936 also resulted in a modification of
the international status of Belgium. King Leopold in an address to his cabinet on October 14, 1936, said, "The reoccupa-
tion of the Rhine by breaking the Locarno agreements both in
the letter and in the spirit has placed us almost in the same
international position as we were in before the War."[63] Any
policy of alliance with a single country would weaken Belgium's position abroad and cause divisions at home. A mere
defensive alliance would not be sufficient, since aid could not
arrive in time to bear the brunt of an attack. "That is why,"
King Leopold continued, "we must follow a policy exclusively
and entirely Belgian. This policy should aim resolutely at

[60] Same, No. 180, 1938, pp. 10-13.   [61] Same, 11.
[62] Same, 1938, pp. 368-75.
[63] For the documents relative to the new policy of Belgium, see Royal Institute of International Affairs, *Documents on International Affairs, 1936*, 250-51.

placing us outside any dispute of our neighbors. It responds to our national ideal."

It was subsequently explained that this speech, which was devoted primarily to a justification for Belgian rearmament, did not mean that Belgium wished to renounce the League of Nations and revert to the prewar status of neutrality. What Belgium wanted was to be free from obligations to render military assistance to another state, and secondly, to make an independent examination of any new agreement for a Western pact to replace the Locarno treaties. After a period of negotiations, there was signed on April 24, 1937, a joint Anglo-French declaration which released Belgium from her obligations under the Locarno treaties and the Four-Power Agreement of March 19, 1936. France and Great Britain reaffirmed their own obligations under the Locarno agreements and renewed their pledges of assistance to Belgium in the event of attack, while the latter undertook to defend her frontier against aggression and gave assurances of loyalty to the Covenant of the League.

The Netherlands government also joined the movement toward "*de facto* revision" of the Covenant. Its delegate stated on January 31, 1938, that "the Netherlands Government has never desired, and does not now desire, a return to the old system of general neutrality when a war breaks out. It still supports the system of collective security. But this does not prevent it from looking the facts in the face. The obligation to apply sanctions . . . no longer can be considered . . . as in force. For the moment, there remains the faculty of applying sanctions."[64]

The League of Nations was not slow to take cognizance of the necessity for considering the problems raised by the failure of sanctions. By a resolution of July 4, 1936, the Assembly recommended that the Council invite the members of the League to make proposals for the improvement of the application of the principles of the Covenant and that the Secretary-General be instructed to make a classification of the proposals

[64] League of Nations, *Official Journal,* Special Supplement No. 180, 1938, p. 14.

and report to the next meeting of the Assembly. The problem, as conceived by the Assembly, was expressed in the preamble of the resolution of July 4, 1936, as follows: "Noting that various circumstances have prevented the full application of the Covenant of the League of Nations; Remaining firmly attached to the principles of the Covenant . . . ; Being desirous of strengthening the authority of the League of Nations by adapting the application of these principles to the lessons of experience; Being convinced that it is necessary to strengthen the real effectiveness of the guarantees of security which the League affords to its Members."[65]

By November 20, 1936, communications had been received from twenty-five governments, and seventeen others had made statements in the Assembly. The declarations of these forty-two governments were duly classified and analyzed by the Secretary-General in accordance with the Assembly resolution of July 4.[66]

Some Governments were doubtful about the expediency of considering the application of the principles of the Covenant at the time. Poland, for example, thought that the study was premature and that the discussion should take place "in a political atmosphere which had been cleared of the heavy anxieties of the present moment." The U.S.S.R., on the contrary, expressed the view that "it is the very presence of these anxieties which constitutes the most powerful argument in favour of an early consideration of this question."[67]

The governments stated, in general, that they appreciated the value of the League and desired its maintenance and prosperity, but there was disagreement over functions, obligations, and methods. Some governments tended to emphasize

[65] For the text of the Assembly resolution, see same, No. 154, 1936, p. 6. This was a companion resolution to the one ending sanctions against Italy. For the revisionist movement, see S. Engel, *League Reform: An Analysis of Official Proposals and Discussions, 1936-1939.*

[66] For this classification and analysis, see Engel, 44-97. The communications received are reproduced in the same document (pp. 6-40). For an analysis of the statements, see Georg Schwarzenberger, "The States Members of the League and the Reform of the Covenant," II (1936), 351-59.

[67] League of Nations, *Official Journal*, Special Supplement No. 154, 1936, p. 47.

collective security, prevention of war, or disarmament, but others stressed the necessity of effective application of the Covenant as a whole. A substantial number of governments favored the maintenance or strengthening of the Covenant. Others, however, advocated a restriction of obligations under the Covenant on the ground that formal obligations should more nearly correspond with what could actually be undertaken. Several governments stressed the importance of a genuine intention to apply the Covenant. Most were opposed, or at least not favorable, to the idea of amending the Covenant. Accessory agreements and interpretations by Assembly resolutions were suggested as methods of revision, while Colombia proposed that doubts over the interpretation of the Covenant be settled by the Permanent Court of International Justice, and the New Zealand government recommended that all members of the League hold a national plebiscite on the application of Article 16.

Twenty-two governments referred to the League's lack of universality as an obstacle or expressed the desire that it should be made universal. The Peruvian government wished to make the conditions of admission and withdrawal more strict. The majority of governments desiring the universality of the League declared in favor of regular co-operation with nonmembers. Colombia, Panama, and Uruguay put forth proposals for regional or continental unions to be substituted, to a greater or lesser extent, for the League of Nations, and the French government stated that "it would be a serious mistake to compromise this principle of universality."[68]

Certain governments proposed to change the composition of the Council by abolishing the permanent seats, causing members of the Council to be elected on a regional basis or substituting a system of rotation for election, or combining the two. Argentina and Panama desired an examination of the respective jurisdictions of the Council and Assembly, and Peru advocated proportional representation of continental groups in the organization of the Secretariat.

[68] Same, 61.

The general unanimity rule (Article 5) gave rise to little comment, although it was proposed that in some cases the rule should be interpreted in a particular way; for example, that the votes of the parties to a dispute should not be counted.

With reference to the reduction and limitation of armaments (Article 8) several governments expressed the opinion that new discussions should be undertaken. More specific proposals included the publicity of budgetary expenditures for armaments, supervision of the manufacture of and trade in arms, establishment of a permanent disarmament commission, and creation of an international force.

In connection with Article 11 attention was called to the necessity of preventive action and of League intervention at an early stage. The Russian delegate expressed the opinion that Article 11 cannot "avert a breach of the peace which arises from calculated aggressiveness and the pursuit of conquest, for which disputes are deliberately engineered."[69] Some governments suggested that in procedure under Article 11 the votes of the parties concerned should not be counted or that the rule of unanimity should be abolished. The Bulgarian government proposed that Article 11 be supplemented by bilateral conventions, and several other governments thought that the Convention of September 26, 1931, to Improve the Means of Preventing War should be the complement of Article 11.

There were several proposals, especially from the Argentine government, that the Covenant of the League be co-ordinated with the Pact of Paris and the Argentine Anti-War Treaty.

Several governments made references to an improvement in the methods for pacific settlement of disputes; for example, the development of procedure under Article 13 and the recommendation that decisions to ask the Permanent Court of International Justice for an advisory opinion be taken by a majority vote.

Some general observations on the subject of Article 10 were made, and its relations to Articles 16 and 19 were pointed out.

[69] Same, 68.

Since the failure of action under Article 16 to halt aggression was largely responsible for the discussion of revision of the Covenant, it is interesting to note the statements about that article. The declarations and proposals of several governments indicated that they regarded collective security as one of the most important elements in the Covenant. The view was expressed that application of Article 16 should be contingent on certain conditions. Peru called attention to the disproportion, from the point of view of degree of civilization, often existing between two parties to a dispute—specifically the Italo-Ethiopian conflict. Hungary wanted "the repressive clauses of the Covenant" brought into equilibrium with Articles 11, 13, and 19; New Zealand stressed the importance of a definite method of rectifying international grievances; Denmark, Finland, Norway, Sweden, and Canada referred to the close connection between Articles 8 and 16.

Some governments were doubtful about the practical value of the principle of collective security under the existing circumstances. The Argentine government stated that those provisions of the Covenant no longer in harmony with the realities of international life should be given an optional character. The delegate of Canada said that his government had made no absolute commitments either for or against participation in war or other forms of force and that any decision with regard to such participation would be taken in the light of all existing circumstances. Ecuador referred to a "right of abstention," and Panama and Peru pointed out the difficulty of requiring participation in collective action from states with relatively remote interests in the conflict giving rise to such action. The Swiss government declared that the sanctions system creates inequalities, since sanctions cannot be applied in all cases, and the risks involved are much greater for some states than for others.

With reference to economic and financial sanctions the Swedish government made the general observation that their application depended on general political factors rather than on the adoption of modified texts. Four governments referred to the necessity for making some sort of advance preparations for the application of such measures. The question of economic and financial sanctions raised the problem of whether they should be automatic. The Chinese government declared that measures under Article 16, paragraph 1, should be automatic, immediate, and all-inclusive; Colombia proposed that they come into force automatically as soon as the competent organs of the League had determined the aggressor; and New Zealand expressed the view that sanctions would be ineffective unless they were immediate and automatic, and took the form of a complete boycott. On the other hand, several governments declared against automatic sanctions. Two governments, Peru and the U.S.S.R., suggested that there should be some differentiation among states as to their obligations to apply sanctions.

The Lithuanian government expressed the opinion that sanctions should not be restricted to negative action, but that direct nonmilitary assistance should be given to the victim of aggression. Several other governments referred to the Convention of October 2, 1930, for Financial Assistance. The delegation of Panama proposed "diplomatic and moral" sanctions and compensation for damage caused by aggression.

The question of military sanctions also evoked a diversity of views. The Chinese and Portuguese governments emphasized the utility of this type of action. Most of the governments which expressed an opinion believed that military sanctions should not be universally obligatory. The Argentine government presented a typical view in stating that military measures should not "be binding on Members not implicated in the dispute, or only having an indirect interest therein."[70] The New Zealand government, however, indicated its willingness to join in the collective application of force against any future aggressor, and Colombia stated that military sanctions should be obligatory for states situated in the same continent as the aggressor.

A number of governments were in favor of regional pacts of

[70] Same, 81.

mutual assistance as a device for supplementing the guarantees of the Covenant. There was usually a stipulation that these pacts should satisfy certain conditions; for example, that they should be open to the accession of other states, concluded in conformity with League principles and supervised by the League, and designed to supplement, not weaken, the Covenant. Most of the proposals for the application of Article 16 and regional pacts of mutual assistance would increase the functions of organs of the League in determining the aggressor and applying sanctions.

In addition to the foregoing declarations and proposals there was a variety of comments on other aspects of the Covenant. The Bulgarian government considered it important to co-ordinate Articles 18 and 20 by refusing registration to treaties incompatible with the Covenant. A number of governments declared themselves in varying degrees in favor of the principle of Article 19. Four of the Latin American governments commented on Article 21. Haiti and Iraq wished some sort of re-examination of the mandate system.

There were a substantial number of references to the desirability of certain forms of international co-operation—economic, financial, and "in bringing about a closer understanding between peoples." Several governments wished to separate the Covenant from the Peace Treaties. Finally, Colombia proposed that the Permanent Court of International Justice settle doubts about the interpretation of the Covenant.

The foregoing summary of the comments of forty-two governments on the problems of revising the Covenant points to two conclusions: (a) a wide variety of questions with respect to nearly every part of the Covenant was raised, and (b) the focal point of the comments and proposals was obviously Article 16.

By a resolution of October 10, 1936, the Assembly set up a Special Committee of twenty-eight member states to study the proposals which had been made and to prepare a report.[71] This committee held its first session December 14 to 17, 1936,

[71] Same, 41-43.

to determine its method of work. Bourquin of Belgium was elected chairman, a list of the principal questions raised in the government communications and declarations was drawn up, and a number of *rapporteurs* were instructed to make an analysis of the problems to be examined. On May 31, the *rapporteurs* held an unofficial exchange of views. A meeting of the committee on September 30, 1937, resulted in the framing by a committee of jurists of proposals with regard to the separation of the Covenant from the Peace Treaties; approval of a draft resolution declaring that the League should take steps to co-ordinate its action with states nonmembers of the League, but bound by the Pact of Paris and the Argentine Anti-War Treaty; and approval of a proposal to request suggestions from nonmember states.[72]

The third session of the Special Committee, held January 31 to February 2, 1938, was devoted to an examination and discussion of a report by Lord Cranborne on the participation of all states in the League of Nations.[73] One aspect of this question related to the rules and procedure for the admission of nonmember nations to the League, and a memorandum dealing with this subject was prepared by the Secretariat. The entire report of Viscount Cranborne was devoted to the central problem of the universality of the League.[74]

The Cranborne report was an analysis of the situation, summarizing all points of view, rather than an argument for any one position. Universal membership in the League, this report stated, might mean the inclusion of all politically organized territory, all states to which membership was open under Article 1 of the Covenant, or all nations whose participation was essential to any genuine scheme of international co-operation; or more immediately, it might mean the extension of League membership to those states which were nonmembers and whose co-operation was particularly essential.

The grounds for the desirability of universal membership in the League were (a) that the conceptions on which the League was based implied universality as an ideal; (b) that the Cove-

[72] Same, No. 180, 1938, p. 5.   [73] Same, 5-60.   [74] Same, 41 ff.

nant was framed on the assumption that the League would be universal and could not function effectively otherwise; and (c) that lack of universality engendered the danger of a system of alliances and division into rival armed camps.[75]

In answer to the question of why League membership was not universal, three classes of nonmembers were identified. First, some states were opposed to the idea of general international co-operation as such and wished to maintain their international contacts on an *ad hoc* basis. Second, some nations were not opposed to the general idea of international co-operation but hesitated to assume definite commitments. Third, other states fell in neither of the two other classes but disapproved of certain features of the League as constituted.

Considerations of the importance and feasibility of obtaining universal membership led to a discussion of the three possible types of organization for the League, with the implications of each type. First, a league of nations might provide for the actual enforcement of peace by the imposition of sanctions in some form. This, stated the Cranborne report, might be called a "coercive" league. As an alternative, there might be a league involving no obligation whatever to impose sanctions. Machinery for the pacific settlement of international disputes would be provided, but failure to use it or abide by its decisions would involve no commitments on the part of third members to use force to deter a delinquent state. This type of league would be "noncoercive." A third type would be an "intermediate" league, which would avoid obligations for a definite and predetermined course in the event of aggression. As each threatening situation arose, the members would meet and consult. Decisions would be on an *ad hoc* basis, and the possibility of coercive action would not be excluded. Third members of such a league would have a right,[76] but not a duty, to impose sanctions, although there might be some regulation of the use of coercion. In the words of the report, "One of the legal

[75] In a summary of opinions with respect to functioning of the League if membership were universal, it was pointed out that universality would not guarantee effectiveness.

[76] The report used the word "faculty."

effects of giving such a faculty would be that no member which had violated the Covenant could, as a matter of juridical right, complain of the use of force against it by other members, or require of these the observance of the rules of neutrality in the dispute involved."[77]

If the device of an "intermediate" league were adopted and sanctions were made "facultative" instead of obligatory—and this would seem to be a temptingly plausible compromise—the modification of Article 16 would go beyond the previously prevailing interpretation. Formerly, the application of sanctions was incumbent upon members of the League in case of a "resort to war" within the meaning of Article 16; only the existence of such a situation was open to the decision of the members. In an "intermediate" league the obligation itself would be replaced by a permissive grant. The "shall" of Article 16 would be changed to "may."

The discussion of the Cranborne report by the Special Committee reflected the fundamental dilemma involved in its terms of reference. The League of Nations must be "universal" to function effectively, but it could be made universal, if at all, only by eliminating from the Covenant all obligations which gave it practical meaning. One might say, paradoxically, that so far as the restraint of aggression was concerned, the League could be effective only by satisfying two mutually exclusive conditions. And this would be merely to say that the League under the circumstances could not be depended upon to control international violence. In the words of the Cranborne report,

those whose ideal is a more or less coercive League, and who want universal membership in order to make such a League effective, are confronted with the possibility that the principal condition on which alone this ideal can be realised can perhaps only be achieved by sacrificing a large part of the ideal itself. Those, on the other hand, whose ideal is a non-coercive League, for the reason, amongst others, that universal membership would thereby be facilitated, must not overlook the possibility that the achievement of it in these

[77] League of Nations, *Official Journal*, Special Supplement No. 180, 1938, p. 42.

conditions might add little to the world which it would not have possessed without a League at all.[78]

The prevailing attitude of the members of the Special Committee was that the letter of the Covenant could not be carried out under the prevailing conditions, but that the idea of collective security should not be abandoned for the future.

The Special Committee came to no decision for a proposed course of action and restricted itself to transmitting to the Assembly a brief report of progress, with the minutes of its meeting and the reports submitted by its *rapporteurs*.[79] The committee had an unenviable task. Difficulties arising from a denial of the basic postulates of collective security could not be overcome by devising a slightly different form of collective security. Little could reasonably be expected from an attempt to remedy an indisposition to apply the Covenant by tinkering with its machinery. Particular defects of the Covenant were irrelevant to the larger question. Efforts to eliminate those defects were entirely in order, but the fundamental problem was the nonuse, not the imperfection, of the instrument. A sufficient juridical and organizational basis of collective security existed. The difficulty lay in the political, social, economic, and ideological spheres.

An analysis of the trend of opinion, undertaken by the New Commonwealth Institute, pointed up the dilemmas involved in a *"de facto* revision" of the Covenant. One report analyzing the statements of governments on the subject of revision of the Covenant was issued in December, 1936.[80] A second report (December, 1937) was concerned with an analysis of the work

[78] Same, 43.

[79] In addition to the Cranborne report, these included discussions of the coordination of peace instruments, regional or continental organization of the League, methods of revision, and Articles 10, 11, and 16. Same, 76 ff. In September, 1938, the Assembly adopted a resolution to refer a report of the Sixth Committee, relating to Article 16, to the members of the League, a resolution endorsing co-operation between the League and nonmember states, and a resolution recommending the separation of the Covenant from the Peace Treaties. A resolution providing that recommendations might be made under Article 11, paragraph 1, without the consent of the parties to a dispute was defeated, with Hungary and Poland voting in the negative, and eleven states abstaining (same, No. 183, 1938, pp. 97-100, 142-52).

[80] Schwarzenberger, II, 351-59.

of the League's Special Committee and concluded: "To re-capitulate—the first part of our survey has shown how under the unanimity rule of the Covenant, the League machinery for the repression of aggression can be reduced to a more theoretical existence and how as a result, a *de facto* revision of the League, transforming it into a non-coercive League, has in fact taken place. In the Reform Committee the struggle still continues between those forces which want to see a legal seal on this *de facto* situation and those which wish to leave the door open for a return to the full application of the Cove-nant."[81]

In order to obtain the opinions of qualified students of this question, it was decided to send a questionnaire to a number of specially chosen collaborators all over the world, excepting Germany, Italy, and Japan. Replies were received from men in public life and authorities on international law and relations of fourteen different nationalities.[82] Unanimity was nearly reached on the proposition that there had been a *"de facto* revision" of the Covenant, and most collaborators denied that the attitude of League members was consistent with their legal obligations. The majority felt that any alteration in the text of the Covenant would, under the circumstances, mean a retrogression rather than a reform.

There was substantial agreement that a connection existed between hostilities in different regions and that little faith could be placed in the device of localizing war. Authorities on international law were convinced that the collective method was better than "individual peace."

Many of the replies stressed the importance of conditions indispensable to a genuine system of international justice and security. A relatively high percentage favored a short-term solution similar to the ideas of Winston Churchill, according to which the peace system would be based on a defensive alliance between Great Britain, France, possibly the U.S.S.R.,

---

[81] Same, III (1937), 271-72.

[82] For an analysis of these replies, see Georg Schwarzenberger, "An Analysis of the Replies to Our Questionnaire on the *De Facto* Revision of the Covenant," 60-74.

and any other League members desiring to participate. This system, it was claimed, would have a great superiority of force, homogeneity of interest, and the benevolent neutrality of the United States. It would also provide a method for peaceful change between members and would be open to adherence by other states.

Numerous replies pointed out that methods existed to prevent the outbreak of a major war, but that the question was one of whether governments would avail themselves of these opportunities. The majority believed that security should come before redress of grievances and disarmament, but many emphasized the point that they must be dealt with simultaneously. The following paragraphs, selected from the many expressions of contemporary opinion toward this dilemma, state clearly the predicament of the times:

Statesmen, backed to a large extent by public opinion, have come to the conclusion that it is simpler, safer and less costly, to keep *individually* out of war, to re-arm to the best of their ability and means, so as to divert aggression to a more vulnerable victim—and for the rest, to hope for the best.[83]

For the present [1939] I think our course of action in regard to the League is clear. We should recognise the fact that main negotiations must take place outside the League, and that a method which would have been right in relation to one issue in 1935 may be wrong, and dangerously wrong, in relation to other issues, under different conditions, in 1939. We should, however, keep the League organisation active. . . .

Rigidly to oppose every act inconsistent with the Covenant . . . would inevitably, in the actual political and strategic conditions [in 1939], involve immediate war on a large scale with no very good prospects of achieving both victory and a result worth the price.[84]

The phase of disintegration in the principle of concern was characterized by the formal retention of that principle in international organization, together with the disappearance of even a pretext of effective application. Instead of control by the group of conflict among its members, there was the attempt

[83] Schwarzenberger, "The States Members of the League," III, 265.
[84] Arthur Salter, *Security: Can We Retrieve It?*, 169-70.

of each to keep out of trouble and hope for the best. Whatever the necessity and merits of this attitude as a policy, it
was the negation of an institutionalized control of international
conflict.

In one challenge to collective security, remonstrances, conciliation, inquiry, and collective nonrecognition were insufficient to halt the conflict and protect the victim, but the offending member of the League withdrew from the organization.
In another and comparatively minor case, hostilities came to
an uneasy and inconclusive end after long and tedious negotiation, and the offending member likewise withdrew from the
League. In a third case, sanctions under Article 16 were attempted on a timid and limited scale, and the aggressor
secured from the League a recognition of the conquest of the
victim. These three by no means encompass all the incidents
of international conflict from 1933 to 1939. They represent
selected case histories of the trend. And there were no cases
which exhibited a contrary trend.

The basic attitude toward the principle of concern during
this difficult period was epitomized in the concept of neo-
neutrality, meaning neutrality combined with a positive attitude of interest in war prevention as contrasted with the
passivity and impartiality of the traditional concept of neutrality. This was a concept which insisted "upon non-participa-
tion in war while at the same time seeking to make a contribution to war prevention."[85] The first object of policy was
to avoid conflict, preventive measures were welcomed as long
as they were not felt to jeopardize the chances of avoidance,
and hopes of genuine group control were discarded. The
various governments did not repudiate the principle of concern. They paid allegiance to it and explained why they
could not apply it.

The "de facto revision" of the Covenant in effect carried
forward the process of limitation by interpretation which had
taken place early in the history of the League and which had
persisted. It had been recognized that the obligations of the

[85] Philip C. Jessup, foreword to Georg Cohn, Neo-Neutrality, vi.

Covenant were subject to the decision of each member as to
their applicability, to a gradual and partial application, and to
the reservation of the peculiar position of each member. Now
the recognition was sought, and obtained, that *obligations* did
not exist at all, that the measures contemplated by the Covenant were facultative or permissive. Just as the Covenant was
"interpreted" and not amended when limitations were placed
upon the initial acceptance of the principle of concern, it was
revised "*de facto*" and not amended (or formally repudiated)
during the phase of disintegration. In this process it was
obvious that the problem of revision was not one of this or
that specific provision, but that it arose from the existence of
a fundamental situation in which no international machinery
for the international control of international violence could be
made effectively applicable.

4. The Question of a "Turning Point"

International organization between the two World Wars
reflected an acceptance of the principle of concern (1919-
1920), a limitation of the acceptance (1920-1925), a modified
application (1925-1933), and a rejection or disintegration
(1933-1939).[86] The question naturally arises of whether a
decisive event or turning point can be identified in the record.

Different writers have expressed a wide variety of views on
this matter, with a general tendency to place the determining
factors either in the making of the peace after World War I
or in failure to halt the cycle of aggressions beginning in 1931.
Some, however, take an intermediate point of view. The following typical judgments may be cited:

Sigmund Neumann has contended that, "The collective
security system was already lost at Versailles. The drawn-out
and futile discussions over an Anglo-American military guarantee of France's Rhine frontier and the collapse of the Geneva

[86] The periods are ones of substantial emphasis, rather than of exclusive
characteristic.

security system gave ample proof of the fact that France could not put any faith in such over-all schemes."[87]

Ranshofen-Wertheimer made the suggestion, based on attitudes in the Peace Conference and remarks of Lord Robert Cecil, that "the Anglo-American group in Paris did not realize that they had already abandoned any possibility of a viable and effectual international agency."[88]

The German viewpoint, as might be expected, was to put the blame on the settlement made at the end of World War I. Hitler, for example, said in his speech of May 21, 1935, "When in 1919 the Peace of Versailles was dictated to the German people, death sentence was pronounced upon collective co-operation among nations."[89]

In contrast, there was the view that, "The turning-point came in 1931. . . . But the more serious blow came in 1935."[90]

Quincy Wright in 1938 thought that the disintegration of the international community began with the failure to stop Japanese aggression in Manchukuo and that it had reached a point where it could no longer be denied.[91]

Raymond Swing contended that the turning point, in the sense of the last real chance, came as late as the Brussels Conference of 1937.[92]

C. J. Friedrich's opinion is typical of the intermediate point of view. "The year 1923 marked the parting of the ways. English diplomacy and the English public henceforth recognized that something more than the League was necessary. One finds few explicit statements of what that something was or should be. British thought and action show rather clearly that Great Britain was at least glancing at the balance of power as a possible way out. For the time being, it was hard to discover what might produce an effective balance."[93]

---

[87] *The Future in Perspective,* 106. Other statements in the same book seem to modify the idea that the cause was completely lost so early.

[88] *World Organization,* 19-20.

[89] F. J. Berber (ed.), *Locarno: A Collection of Documents,* 128.

[90] John I. Knudson, *A History of the League of Nations,* 355.

[91] Schwarzenberger, "An Analysis of the Replies," 68.

[92] "How We Lost the Peace in 1937," *Atlantic Monthly,* CLXXIX (1947), 33-37.

[93] *Foreign Policy in the Making,* 148-49.

The same writer also stated, "Although recognized by few at the time, balance-of-power politics re-appeared in the middle 'twenties. Its failure became manifest in the portentous events of 1931-33, when Japan seized Manchuria and Germany once again fell under the control of the militarists."[94]

F. P. Walters divided the history of the League into: (a) the years of growth, 1919-1923; (b) the years of stability, 1923-1931; (c) the years of conflict, 1931-1936; and (d) the years of defeat, 1936-1939.[95]

E. H. Carr distinguished four periods in international relations between 1920 and 1939: (a) the period of enforcement, 1920-1924; (b) the period of pacification, 1924-1930; (c) the period of crisis and the return of power politics, 1930-1933; and (d) the re-emergence of Germany and the end of the treaties, 1933-1939.[96]

Reference may also be made to a French writer, Georges Le Brun Keris, who interpreted the history of the League in terms of three great crises—that of the initial period, the constitutional crisis of 1926, and the general crisis commencing in 1930.[97]

In my opinion, to the extent that a turning point can be identified, it came with the rejection of the Geneva Protocol in 1925—the last real attempt to transfer the controlling decision to an instrumentality of the more inclusive group. Rejection of the Geneva Protocol demonstrated that the principle of concern was not to be incorporated in international organization in any way that would be significant for asserting group homogeneity in the control of conflict among the constituent members. It only required a major test to reveal the actual locus of controlling decisions[98] and to set a precedent for a series of aggressions culminating in World War II.

[94] War: The Causes, Effects, and Control of International Violence, 55-56.

[95] A History of the League of Nations, I, vii-xv.

[96] International Relations between the Two World Wars, 1919-1939, v-vii.

[97] Les Projets de Reforme de la Société des Nations et le Developpement du Pacte, 6.

[98] Note that the rejection of the Geneva Proctocol put collective security on a regional basis and that the Far East was not in the "region" of any of the leading members of the League. Hamilton Fish Armstrong has referred to the

Failure to institutionalize any significant procedure of control through the more inclusive group left the maintenance of peace to the national policies and the alliances of the individual states. This distinction was blurred because national policies could still be expressed to some extent through the techniques and procedures of the League. For the same reason, the chronology relative to the principle of concern in international organization would not necessarily follow the chronology of actual disruptions of the peace. The various national policies might result in the maintenance of peace for a varying length of time even though the principle of concern were not accepted. Reliance on self-help is not equivalent to perpetual conflict. Nevertheless, a combination of conflict situations, inadequacy of self-help to control them, and rejection of the principle of concern can have only one outcome.

Geneva Protocol as the real turning point in the history of the League. *Foreign Affairs*, XXVI (1947), 4.

CHAPTER SIX

Reaffirmation: The United Nations

THE ALLIED victory over the Axis powers in World War II brought a new question about the nature and basis of international legal and political organization for the future. The answer was the United Nations, anticipated and planned during the war, and brought into existence through a Charter signed in 1945. The League of Nations belongs to history, but the United Nations is a crucial issue of the moment. For the United Nations the time span is so short, the events are so close, and the ultimate result is so uncertain, that no definitive statements can be attempted. There is adequate basis, however, for inquiring about the relationship of the new organization to the principle of concern. How does the United Nations compare with the League in this respect? It will be recognized at once that close and rigorous analogies are inappropriate and likely to be misleading. The two international organizations, while similar in many important respects, also reveal some important differences, and in any case the world situation of the 1950's is unique, as was that of the 1920's and the 1930's. What is called for, therefore, is not an item-by-item comparison, but an examination of experience since 1945 in terms of its own characteristic development.

The Charter of the United Nations expresses a vigorous reaffirmation of the principle of concern as the basis of contemporary international organization. The preamble avers the determination "to save succeeding generations from the scourge of war" and "to unite our strength to maintain international peace and security." Prominent among the stated purposes is that of taking effective collective measures for the prevention and removal of threats to the peace and for the suppression of "acts of aggression or other breaches of the peace." One of the principles subscribed to by all the members of the United Nations is that international disputes shall be settled "by peaceful means in such a manner that international peace and security, and justice, are not endangered." It is provided that the principle of nonintervention in matters essentially of domestic jurisdiction shall not prejudice the application of enforcement measures. The Charter even extends the principle of concern beyond the membership of the United Nations by asserting an obligation to prevent nonmembers from jeopardizing international peace and security (Article 2, paragraph 6).

The General Assembly of the United Nations is authorized to deal with any questions relating to international peace and security—a broad mandate indeed. In case of any dispute "the continuance of which is likely to endanger the maintenance of international peace and security," the parties concerned have an obligation to seek a solution by a pacific means. The Security Council has the duty of intervening to expedite a settlement at any stage which it deems necessary. If enforcement action is called for, the Security Council "shall determine the existence of any threat to the peace, breach of the peace, or act of aggression and shall make recommendations, or decide what measures shall be taken . . . to maintain or restore international peace and security" (Article 39). Thus, the dominant conception of the Charter is that any disruption of international peace is a matter of concern to all members of the United Nations.

All the nations represented at the San Francisco Conference ratified the Charter and became original members of the United Nations. Although universal membership has not been attained, all the Great Powers have been members from the beginning. Thus, the kind of geographical limitation which was so serious for the League of Nations did not recur for the new organization.

1. INTERPRETATION

The United Nations has tended to take a broad view of its own competence under the Charter. The General Assembly's authority to discuss and to make recommendations covers the entire question of world peace, while the Security Council has the "primary responsibility" of maintaining international peace and security. Thus, anything which constitutes a "threat to the peace, breach of the peace, or act of aggression" is brought within the orbit of the United Nations. The principal "reserve clause" limiting this delegation of authority is the provision of Article 2, paragraph 7, "Nothing contained in the present Charter shall authorize the United Nations to intervene in matters which are essentially within the domestic jurisdiction of any state or shall require the members to submit such matters to settlement under the present Charter."

A relatively broad or narrow range for the jurisdiction of the United Nations clearly depends upon the interpretation given to the scope of its chief function as limited by this reserve clause. In practice the tendency has been to follow a broad interpretation and to give primacy to the responsibilities of the United Nations rather than to the limitations upon its authority.[1] When the Indonesian case was brought before the Security Council in 1947, the government of the Netherlands argued strongly that the relation of Indonesia to the Netherlands was a matter essentially of domestic jurisdiction and that the military action was of no concern to the Security Council since it constituted a domestic police action rather than a breach of international peace. Other members took the position that the Indonesian Republic had been given *de facto* recognition, thereby gaining an international standing, and that the situation actually was a breach of the peace within the meaning of the Charter. The question of jurisdiction was not

[1] Authoritative sources for following the work of the United Nations are, in addition to the official documents, the *Yearbook of the United Nations, Annual Reports of the Secretary-General,* and the *United Nations Bulletin* (now the *Review*).

explicitly decided by the Security Council, but it proceeded to deal with the situation on the assumption that it had a competence to act.

During its first session the General Assembly was asked to consider the treatment of persons of Indian origin in the Union of South Africa. The government of India charged that this group had been discriminated against and that such measures violated agreements between the two countries and were contrary to the principles of the United Nations Charter concerning human rights and freedoms. The Union of South Africa argued, on the other hand, that the treatment of its own nationals was a question essentially of domestic jurisdiction, that there were no applicable bilateral international agreements, and that the principles of the Charter did not by themselves create an obligation respecting particular individual liberties. The General Assembly did not formally decide the question of jurisdiction, but it did adopt a resolution which stated that the situation was one which impaired friendly relations between two states and that the treatment of the Indian miniority in the Union of South Africa should be in conformity with international obligations. By passing the resolution, the General Assembly acted on the assumption that it had some competence in the matter, and it implicitly followed the principle that a question normally of domestic jurisdiction becomes one of international concern if it impairs friendly relations among states.

The Spanish and Czechoslovak cases raised questions involving the internal governmental regime of a state. The Security Council dealt with the question of Franco Spain in 1946. The Soviet Union and Poland argued that the very existence of a government established with aid of the Axis aggressor constituted a threat to peace and therefore that definite measures should be taken to overthrow it. Other members of the Security Council felt that while the Franco regime was a "potential menace" to international peace and security, it did not constitute a "breach of the peace" within the meaning of Article 39 of the Charter. The General Assembly then discussed the question and passed a resolution, later modified, barring Franco Spain from membership in international agencies and conferences connected with the United Nations and recommending the recall of ambassadors from Madrid. It was clear from the proceedings in both the Security Council and the General Assembly that the reservation of domestic jurisdiction was not controlling if a decision should be reached that the internal governmental regime constituted a breach of, or threat to, international peace.

When the Communist seizure of power in Czechoslovakia was brought to the attention of the Security Council in 1948, it was the Soviet Union which claimed that a change in governmental regime was a matter of domestic jurisdiction. The United States representative argued that this would be true only if there had been no assistance, direct or indirect, from a foreign power and if there had been no threat of force or other external interference with the political independence of Czechoslovakia. A proposal to appoint a Security Council subcommittee to investigate the situation was lost on account of the negative vote of the Soviet Union, and the case was not taken up by the General Assembly.

The ultimate significance of the limitation concerning matters of domestic jurisdiction is not clear as yet. This provision has been invoked at various times in support of a restrictive interpretation of the Charter, but it has not proved to be a serious limitation on the work of the United Nations. The approach to an interpretation has not been a technical or legalistic one. When this issue has been raised, the organs of the United Nations "have quite clearly been concerned with the attainment of the major objectives and purposes of the United Nations and have shown an unwillingness to accept any interpretation of Article 2 (7) which would prevent action from being taken in a situation deemed to be of international concern in terms of these purposes."[2]

The original conception was that the peace treaties with the

[2] Leland M. Goodrich and Edvard Hambro, *Charter of the United Nations: Commentary and Documents*, 121.

enemy states would be concluded by the Allies at the end of World War II and that the United Nations would have the responsibility of maintaining peace and security thereafter. Article 107 of the Charter provided, "Nothing in the present Charter shall invalidate or preclude action, in relation to any state which during the Second World War has been an enemy of any signatory to the present Charter, taken or authorized as a result of that war by the Governments having responsibility for such action."

As disagreement among the victors precluded the achievement of stable postwar settlements, it became necessary for the United Nations to function in a different situation from that which had been contemplated. The interpretation of Article 107 therefore became significant for the scope of United Nations activity, especially when new disputes arose over the basis for dealing with unsettled old ones. If all such cases were kept from the United Nations, its competence to deal with threats to the peace would be restricted. This, however, did not occur. When the Korean situation was referred to the General Assembly in 1947, the Soviet Union argued that consideration was barred by Article 107, which was intended to leave with the victors in the war the determination of the terms of peace and the necessary control measures. The position taken by the General Assembly was that Article 107 was permissive and therefore did not bar action through the United Nations.

The same question arose in the Security Council over the Berlin blockade in 1948. The Soviet Union claimed that the solution of problems relating to Germany was a matter for the governments responsible for military occupation and that the Council of Foreign Ministers had been set up to deal with the settlement of all issues related to former enemy countries. The United States, on the other hand, took the position that the immediate question did not deal with Germany as a former enemy state but with the threat to international peace and security growing out of the relations among the occupying powers. The Berlin blockade was lifted, not by direct action of the Security Council, but as the result of a series of informal negotiations.

It is safe to conclude that Article 107 of the Charter does not of itself restrict the competence of the United Nations in dealing with the maintenance of international peace and security. Whether or not a given situation constitutes an existing threat to peace, rather than what has been the history of the dispute, is the important consideration.

Other provisions in the Charter have also been interpreted in a manner consistent with a broad scope for the United Nations. For example, Article 73 (e) requires the transmission of information on nonself-governing territories. Despite the objection of some of the countries concerned, upon the basis of this provision and its general powers of discussion the General Assembly has established a committee to consider the information received and to make recommendations to the governments responsible for the administration of dependent territories. Since these governments are in a minority in the General Assembly, they often find themselves being critically examined on matters which they consider to be in the area of domestic jurisdiction.

Another interesting case of Charter interpretation concerns the voting procedure in the Security Council. Article 27 of the Charter provides that on matters other than procedural, decisions shall be made by an affirmative vote of seven members, "including the concurring votes of the permanent members." This was designed to insure that substantive decisions of the Security Council would not be taken without unanimity among the Great Powers. From the language it might be assumed that a definite affirmative vote of each permanent member would be necessary. That, however, has not been the interpretation in practice. Decisions have been taken if there were at least seven affirmative votes and if no permanent members actually cast a negative vote. This has considerably abated the rigors of the unanimity requirement and reduced the use and "abuse" of the veto, since it has been possible for the Security Council to make decisions when a permanent member was neither willing to vote for a resolution nor yet determined to block its adoption if a sufficient majority of other members favored it.[3] By extension of the same reasoning, an absence from a meeting is considered to have the same effect as an abstention. Therefore, a veto cannot be cast by the simple expedient of boycotting a meeting. A "concurring vote" is deemed to exist unless there is a positive indication of non-concurrence. The importance of these interpretations is shown by the fact that a Security Council decision was possible in the Korean case of June, 1950, when otherwise the resolution before the Council would have been blocked in the absence of an actual affirmative vote by the Soviet Union.

During the latter part of 1950 the "Uniting for Peace" resolution was adopted by the General Assembly. The essence of this resolution lay in its provision that if the Security Council, because of lack of unanimity of the permanent members, failed to exercise its primary responsibility for the maintenance of international peace and security in any apparent threat to the peace, breach of the peace, or act of aggression, the General Assembly should consider the matter immediately with a view to making appropriate recommendations for collective measures, including the use of armed force when necessary. It must be noted that such decisions would be *recommendations,* not binding legal obligations, and that recourse to the General Assembly would not overcome the disunity among the Great Powers. Nevertheless, a procedure was supplied by which the United Nations might act when the occasion arose and a sufficient number of its members were able and willing to do so. Through the "Uniting for Peace" resolution the United Nations gave primacy to its major objective and responsibility for the maintenance of peace, rather than to a specific set of procedural and organizational arrangements.

Even though the organs of the United Nations have followed a broad interpretation of their competence under the Charter, the controlling decisions remain with the member states. The

[3] Goodrich and Hambro, 213-27; Amry Vandenbosch and Willard N. Hogan, *The United Nations,* 145-50.

General Assembly's recommendations may, and often do, have strong practical force, but the question of their acceptance and implementation still lies with the members. The Security Council, on the other hand, has the constitutional authorization to make binding decisions. However, the voting procedure is such that no such decision can be made without the "concurrence" of the permanent members. The result is that on any question of enforcement action each of the Great Powers "decides for itself." In the Korean case the Security Council resolutions took the forms of a determination that the North Korean attack constituted a breach of the peace and recommendations calling upon members of the United Nations to come to the assistance of the Republic of Korea. The major reason for putting the resolutions in this form was that the Security Council had no military forces under its own command. Although Article 43 of the Charter provided that armed forces and facilities would be made available by agreement between the Security Council and the members of the United Nations, no such agreements had been made because of the "cold war." In any case, the arrangements contemplated by Article 43 indicate that the controlling decisions about the armed forces at the disposal of the Security Council were to be made by the member states.

Since the United Nations is an association of sovereign states and not a separate level of governmental authority, its decisions and actions depend upon the co-operation of a sufficient number of its members. No authoritative definitions are provided for such concepts as threats to the peace, breaches of the peace, and acts of aggression. It is not always easy to draw a firm line between a "threat to the peace" within the meaning of the Charter and a "potential (or actual) menace" to peace. Opinions may differ on whether the unrest in French North Africa in 1953, for example, should be construed as a threat to international peace sufficient to take the case out of the category of essentially domestic jurisdiction. Also, one might wonder why the military conflict between North and South Koreans had been promptly referred to the United Nations, but the fighting in Indo-China had persisted for years before being brought to that forum. When does an internal conflict or civil war become a threat to or breach of international peace? This question will have to be answered for each case as it arises, and no doubt the basic significance of each case in relation to the international political situation will be the controlling point. Although there is room for disagreement on whether the United Nations should or should not take up certain cases, the record on the whole has been a positive one. There has been comparatively little evasion of responsibility by narrow and arbitrary interpretation of the organization's mandate.

2. THE PROBLEM OF IMPLEMENTATION

The United Nations has a record of broad interpretation of its own constitutional authority. However, to make decisions and to carry them out effectively are two different things. The major difficulty and principal frustration for the United Nations have been in the problem of implementation, that is to say, in the practical application to the existing international situation. Since the United Nations is an associative organization of member states retaining the principle of "sovereign equality," it has neither the means nor the authority to enforce its own decisions through its own machinery. Therefore, the practical effectiveness of United Nations decisions depends upon a common agreement to implement its presuppositions and the development of supporting national policies.

These prerequisites have been achieved to some extent, but far from completely. East-West tensions and the formation of hostile blocs preclude the agreement and joint action needed to provide the foundation for a stable peace. A big "cold war" and a series of little "hot wars" are incompatible with general co-operation against acts of aggression and threats to the peace. The major test which the United Nations received in the first eight years of its existence was the Korean case. If the permanent members of the Security Council—the United States, Great

Britain, France, China, and the Soviet Union—had been in accord on the handling of this case, the two contending regimes in Korea could not have constituted a threat to world peace, whatever the implications for Korea itself. The situation which actually existed, however, found the United States taking the lead in resisting the North Korean aggressors, with the support of Great Britain and France (both heavily occupied elsewhere); with the Soviet Union friendly and helpful to the aggressors; and with the mainland of China under the control of a regime which put armies in the field against the United Nations forces. The act of aggression was resisted and thwarted, but by military conflict rather than by acceptance and implementation of the Security Council decision by all parties concerned.

Lack of co-operation among the Great Powers is not the only problem in effecting the purposes and authority of the United Nations. There is also the defiance of the smaller countries on some matters. The Union of South Africa, for example, refuses to accept the recommendation of the General Assembly on the question of its nationals of Indian origin and on the former mandate of Southwest Africa. Also, the proposal for the internationalization of Jerusalem has been rejected by both the Jews and the Arabs. On the Kashmir question India and Pakistan have co-operated with the Security Council to some extent, but neither has shown an inclination to surrender its own basic viewpoint. These examples serve as reminders that even if Great Power unanimity existed, there would still be a problem of implementing the decisions made by United Nations organs.

The absence of adequate co-operation in the acceptance and enforcement of United Nations decisions has had important consequences. First, there has been a decreased reliance upon the United Nations as the primary guarantor of international peace and of national security. This does not mean that the United Nations has lost its importance or that for practical purposes it has been reduced to a cipher, but that its significance and impact have been fundamentally changed. There are many complexities and intangibles, but one cannot look closely at the record since 1945 without coming to the conclusion that the United Nations has been a real force in many situations. It serves an important function as a meeting place between East and West, as an instrument for multilateral negotiations, and as an agency with substantial effects and implications in practical international politics.

The United Nations has been a constructive factor in such disputes as those concerning Palestine, Indonesia, Kashmir, and Korea. Through efforts of the General Assembly and the Security Council, with the support of member states, fighting has been stopped or prevented and force has been used against overt aggression. One of the useful aspects of the United Nations is that it sometimes provides a device for escaping an impasse. In connection with the Berlin blockade, for example, the negotiations which relaxed the tension began with a conversation in the delegate's lounge at Lake Success, after all other avenues seemed to be blocked. When the peace treaty with Italy was being written, no agreement could be reached in the Council of Foreign Ministers on the disposition of the former Italian colonies. This deadlock was broken only by an agreement to refer the matter to the General Assembly, with the undertaking to accept its recommendation as binding. Incidentally, the final decision of the General Assembly was different from the various proposals originally supported by the Great Powers.

The existence and activities of the United Nations put the question of peace and war in a changed context. The obligations of the Charter, the automatic conferences, the work of the Secretariat, the debates—all combine to emphasize multilateral diplomacy and to alter the stage on which governments deal with each other. The United Nations provides techniques which would not otherwise be available for easing the transition to independence for a colonial people or for providing a more acceptable means for channeling capital investment to underdeveloped areas. Even in the case of an act of aggression, as in Korea, the situation probably would have been quite different if defense of South Korea had been undertaken by a unilateral national decision of the United States. With all this, however, it remains true that under conditions of international tension and East-West hostility, security cannot be guaranteed by the United Nations but must also be sought through national strength and the formation of alliances. General co-operation becomes a desirable but limited possibility, rather than the chief method for the maintenance of international peace and security.

Second, there has been a shift in emphasis from the Security Council to the General Assembly. When the Charter was drafted, the former was given the "primary responsibility" for the maintenance of international peace and security. However, the Security Council has never received military forces of its own, and in any case, it cannot even make a substantive decision if one of the permanent members chooses to exercise its veto privilege. Effective operation of the Security Council depends upon the principle of unanimity, requiring co-operation among the Big Five. When threats to peace and acts of aggression occur and the necessary co-operation is not forthcoming, the Security Council is not in a position to exercise its "primary responsibility." The General Assembly, on the other hand, can deal with such situations and make recommendations by a two-thirds vote. Consequently, the United Nations can act when a sufficient majority of its members is able and willing to do so. The shift in the organizational center of gravity reached an extreme form in 1953. Although the Charter requires the Security Council to be organized so as to be able to function continuously, it held few meetings during that year and the truce in Korea was referred directly to the General Assembly.

Third, regional security arrangements have developed as the primary form of international co-operation for the protection of national security, in contrast to the essentially universalist concept of the United Nations Charter. The Organization of American States, the North Atlantic Treaty Organization, the Soviet security sphere, the Arab League, and other regional arrangements developed as security for a given group of countries against actual or assumed threats from other groups. Article 51 of the Charter recognizes that "collective self-defense" in the event of an armed attack is valid until the Security Council has taken measures necessary to maintain international peace and security. Arrangements such as NATO therefore can be brought within the framework of the Charter, but they assume importance only when partners on the Security Council feel that they must protect themselves against each other. The impossibility of effectively implementing the universalist assumptions of general international co-operation under existing conditions gives occasion for regional groupings designed to increase security by combined efforts and, in the long run, to strengthen the general organization by helping to discourage acts of aggression.

Fourth, there has been a growing tendency to invoke the principle of self-help in some form. Peoples who are disillusioned by the experiences in attempting international co-operation for the maintenance of peace may react with the slogan of "going it alone." National military strength is relied on, and if another country is seen as a serious threat, the attempt is made to build up a margin of armaments to provide security. The whole process of international tensions, threats to national security, and an armament race is accompanied by feelings of frustration and anger and by strong expressions of nationalism. The attitudes thus aroused in turn make it more difficult to organize security on the basis of international co-operation. The phenomenon now known as "neutralism" is also an expression of the principle of self-help in that it implicitly denies the assumptions of co-operation in the maintenance and enforcement of peace. If an international organization is committed to act against aggression, the members cannot well be "neutral" between an aggressor and the victim, nor toward those who are attempting to restrain the former and protect the latter. Yet the policies of some governments seemed to reflect the idea that the enforcement action in Korea was merely a conflict between two rival alliances with which they had no direct concern. It is true that the dwarfs are in danger when the giants are battling, and naturally they do not relish the necessity of "taking sides." This painful dilemma, however, does not arise under the assumption of Great Power unanimity. Without the East-West conflict, there would be no occasion for "neutralism" to develop.

The basic problem of the United Nations lies in the fact that implementation and enforcement of its decisions depend upon supporting national policies and co-operative action by the members, and these have not been forthcoming to a sufficient extent. Yet the United Nations cannot achieve the desired result by fiat, nor can it directly carry out its own decisions. The contrast between this situation and that of the League of Nations, which interpreted its own authority much more narrowly, lies in the willingness of a majority of the members of the United Nations to attempt an enforcement of the provisions of the Charter.

3. THE DILEMMA OF COLLECTIVE SECURITY

The term "collective security" has often been used with reference to the League of Nations and the United Nations, although it does not occur in either the Covenant or the Charter. Frequent use in both scholarly and popular literature concerning international relations has made the expression familiar—apparently quite simple and almost self-explanatory. Attempts to frame a precise definition, however, reveal that the concept is complex and illusive. Perhaps the best way to approach a clarification is to suggest a definition and then to give a brief explanation of what is meant by the definition. Collective security, then, refers to "general co-operative action for the maintenance and enforcement of international peace." Collective security involves, first of all, an acceptance of the principle of concern. It presupposes that every state has an interest in the occurrence of international conflict and in the methods by which international disputes are settled. There-

fore, the idea that war is a fact outside the realm of law, together with reliance on the principle of self-help as a basis for
international organization, is incompatible with a collective
security system.

Collective action, if necessary to maintain or restore peace,
is also involved. Not all collective action, however, can be
described as collective security. For example, the members
of an alliance in a balance-of-power system take collective
action among themselves against a rival alliance. The reference to *general* co-operative action indicates that the overwhelming majority must unite against an aggressor. Under
a collective security system, reliance is placed on a preponder-
ance of power exercised through the instrumentalities of the
international community, rather than on a balancing of power
among rival groupings of nations.[4]

The word "action" includes the various techniques of pacific
settlement and does not refer solely to the application of
forcible sanctions. Collective security, therefore, is not synonymous with military action, but it does imply a resort to
force if other means are inadequate to prevent aggression.
If this were not so, co-operative action for the maintenance
of peace would be thwarted at the first serious and determined
challenge. Collective security may be expressed through efforts
to prevent war, but it potentially involves the use of force to
restore peace if aggression occurs.

Much of the confusion over the term "collective security"
arises from a failure to distinguish between its use as an
objective, a condition, and a method. The purpose, of course,
is to achieve a situation under which acts of aggression and
other breaches of the peace will not occur. If this *objective* is
reached, the world would then be in a *condition* of collective
security. Sometimes the principle is criticized because this
condition has not been reached either under the League of
Nations or the United Nations. This, however, is not conclusive, as can easily be shown by a simple analogy. *National*

---

[4] For a statement of the contrasting assumptions involved, see Wright, *A
Study of War*, II, 781-83.

security is not actually achieved in a situation of serious international tensions, yet it remains a valid primary objective. It seems preferable to think of "collective security" as a method of reaching an objective. The method is co-operative action based on the principle of concern; the objective is a stable international order. In other words, collective security may be considered as one way of working toward the goal of national security. Since collective security is sometimes defined in terms of the *machinery* for joint action,[5] it should be understood that the *method* implies the appropriate organizational and procedural means.

Opposition to reliance upon a collective security system such as that contemplated by the Charter of the United Nations comes from three sources. One of these is found in the various groups which reject the basic validity of the principle of concern. This attitude may be exhibited in isolationism (in the true meaning of the term) or in "neutralism" of one kind or another. It may reflect the belief that a Great Power should "go it alone" or that a small country should avoid the danger of taking sides. These are adaptations of the principle of self-help, relying upon national action or upon alliances in the face of immediate threats, but accepting no commitment in the event of a breach of the peace as such.

Another source of opposition is the "world government" school of thought, which holds that peace is incompatible with the continuance of national sovereignty. This approach views the nation-state system as productive of wars and holds that dependence cannot be placed in the co-operative action of sovereign states to preserve the peace. Effective supranational government, therefore, is essential in the nature of the case, and it follows that any lesser collective security system is by definition inadequate.

Finally, some scholars criticize the concept of collective security on the ground that it is in principle unworkable. For example, Hans Morgenthau has stated three assumptions which must be fulfilled if collective security is to operate as a

[5] Georg Schwarzenberger, *Power Politics*, 494.

device for the prevention of war, yet which, he has concluded, cannot be made to work in the contemporary world. These assumptions are that "(1) the collective system must be able to muster at all times such overwhelming strength against any potential aggressor or coalition of aggressors that the latter would never dare to challenge the order defended by the collective system; (2) at least those nations whose combined strength would meet the requirement under (1) must have the same conception of security which they are supposed to defend; (3) those nations must be willing to subordinate whatever conflicting political interests may still separate them to the common good defined in terms of the collective defense of all member states."[6]

The first two of these assumptions are obvious, if a collective security system is to be completely effective. Morgenthau draws the conclusion, however, that the tendency for a conflict of interests between *status quo* and revisionist nations, such as has existed since 1919, means that "the attempt to freeze the particular status quo by means of collective security is in the long run doomed to failure."[7] This conclusion on the impotence of collective security, however, does not take into consideration the nature of the available alternatives. One might make a plausible case that neither unilateral action by individual Great Powers nor a system of balance-of-power alliances is adequate to provide for orderly and peaceful change of a particular *status quo* and that the prerequisites and conditions for an effective world government are not presently available. In such a case, no constructive principle of action would remain. Assumptions about the essentials of an effective collective security system and the recognized difficulties in applying this principle do not preclude the possibility that in some cases an attempt to apply this method may be at least as hopeful as any alternative course of action. The "failure" of the League of Nations has not restored traditional neutrality as a dependable

[6] *Politics among Nations*, 389; cp. also, Frederick L. Schuman, *International Politics*, 127, 235-38, and *The Commonwealth of Man*, 344-420.

[7] P. 390.

basis of international organization, nor has it pointed to reliance on the supranational principle of government.

Morgenthau assumes that the diplomacy of collective security must aim at transforming all local conflicts into world
conflicts and that it will result in spreading wars rather than
preventing them. He approves, instead, of the type of diplomacy which attempts to localize wars, citing the instance of
British efforts in the summer of 1914 to limit the conflict between Austria and Serbia. It is difficult to see how the conclusion drawn from this incident can be prejudicial to the principle of collective security. It seems to indicate that under
modern conditions a war once started is likely to spread and
that the methods of traditional diplomacy are not adequate to
prevent this result. It is the nature of war in modern society,
rather than the principle of collective security, which prevents
the localization of war.

Morgenthau's third assumption is even more questionable.
One of the stated implications is, "Collective security expects
the policies of the individual nations to be inspired by the ideal
of mutual assistance and a spirit of self-sacrifice which will not
shrink even from the supreme sacrifice of war should it be
required by that ideal."[8] First of all, this involves the am-
biguous concept of "national self-interest." It is axiomatic, of
course, that an invasion of a nation, or one of its neighbors,
will be viewed with greater concern than some conflict on the
other side of the globe. Nevertheless, it is not possible in principle to draw a line around a conception of national interest
to exclude the possibility that the start of a war anywhere may
be regarded as a violation of national security interest. Under
a balance-of-power system, factors which tend to upset the
balance are viewed as threats to national interests, especially
by the *status quo* powers. Countries do not wait until an invasion occurs before they begin to form protective alliances,
but take their cue from any situation which seems to contain
the seeds of a future threat. In view of the nature of modern
warfare, is it realistic to say that the American people have

[8] P. 391.

less of a "national interest" in preventing *any* act of aggression from sparking a world conflagration than they had in European policy toward South America in 1823, the Oregon boundary in the 1840's, the Spanish treatment of Cubans in 1898, or the terms upon which certain Latin American countries would satisfy their European creditors?

Was it really to the "national interest" of France and Great Britain in 1935 and 1936 to appease Mussolini in the hope of his co-operation against Hitler? It is not necessary to invoke a spirit of self-sacrificing altruism to condemn the policy expressed in the Hoare-Laval agreement and the hesitancy to apply effective sanctions in the Italo-Ethiopian case. Likewise, one may condemn the neutrality legislation of the 1930's on the grounds that it contributed to the spread of Axis aggression and was therefore contrary to the national interest of the United States. The debacle of collective security during the 1930's was not due to a refusal to subordinate national interests to collective security, but to mistaken conceptions of what was required to protect national interests.

The United States since 1945 has shown a "national interest" in the status of Greece, Turkey, Iran, Palestine, Indonesia, Korea, Austria, Germany, Japan, and a host of other countries. It seems reasonable to suppose that a concern based upon "national interest" would also be shown if, say, Greece should attack Bulgaria, or Italy and Yugoslavia should come to blows over Trieste. Even attacks by our "friends" on our "enemies" would put the "fat in the fire" and perhaps affect us adversely. In fact, it would be difficult to imagine any breach of international peace today in which the United States would not have a "national interest." Or, to take another country, why should Turkey send troops to Korea? In answer, one might refer to its relation with the NATO powers and its concern with Soviet expansion. But if Turkey has a "national interest" in the Korean conflict under the circumstances, the concept does not have to be stretched much further to cover any act of aggression. What collective security requires is not the renunciation of national interests—the forsaking of national egotisms and the national policies serving them. It requires only the *reinterpretation* of the "national interest." There is no valid reason for setting collective security and national interests rigidly in opposition to each other and assuming that the latter must be sacrificed if the former is to exist. It is a matter of enlightened self-interest, rather than of self-sacrificing altruism. As Kenneth W. Thompson has written: "The uses of collective security are more modest and limited than its more ardent advocates appreciate. Yet if participants base their policies on enduring political principles and judge and measure each action by the interests and power involved, it need not be an inevitable blind alley. Between the scylla of blind acceptance and the charybdis of logical rejection we must aim to establish the intellectual foundations required for an empirical and pragmatic approach to the modern concept of collective security."[9]

Collective security is a method of organizing the widest possible co-operation in efforts to maintain international peace and security. Even if the prevailing distribution of power does not permit it to work ideally, applications of the method may make a margin of difference in the handling of international disputes and breaches of the peace. Since 1945 it has been utilized with varying degrees of success. Co-operative action based on the principle of concern has taken place in such serious situations as those in Palestine, Indonesia, and Kashmir. Attempts to "prove" on the basis of arbitrary assumptions that collective security is inherently unworkable are not convincing in the face of the actual use of this method and the achievement of significant, although imperfect, results. It certainly is not clear that better results would automatically ensue from a reliance exclusively upon unilateral diplomacy and the traditional type of alliance.

In the case of Korea, collective security was put to the test of military enforcement. The relative degree of success in terms of long-range objectives is debatable, but there is no disputing the fact that the aggressor did not gain a square

9 "Collective Security Reexamined," 772.

inch of territory by three years of fighting. The results in this case cannot be completely discounted on the ground that the United States took a decisive role because of its own national security interest. The fact remains that the effort was a co-operative one; there is no proof that the situation would have been improved if the United Nations were not in existence and if the United States had intervened as a unilateral act. If the Korean case proves anything concerning national interest and collective security, it seems to point to the fact that the national interest of the United States requires an implementation of methods for general co-operative action to maintain international peace and security.

The United Nations, as a collective security system, represents an acceptance of the principle of concern as a basis for international organization, together with decentralized institutional arrangements for the making and executing of decisions. As in the case of the League of Nations, the controlling decisions and the effective power remain with the constituent members of the more inclusive organization, and the latter does not have any significant authority or means for enforcement directly upon individuals. This is not to say, however, that the United Nations does not have usefulness and possibilities. The real question is to what extent and under what conditions co-operative action for the maintenance of international peace and security is feasible. In any political community, peace and order can be maintained only by the acquiescence and co-operation of the dominant groups within the society. To put it axiomatically, peace necessitates the co-operation of those with power to disrupt the peace. If a sufficient degree of acquiescence and co-operation is not maintained, civil war breaks out or the society is otherwise disrupted. If a society has a government effectively incorporating the principle of concern, there exists an authority more inclusive and more powerful than any of the competing groups within that society. This is true of the typical contemporary nation-state. In the absence of such a superior authority, however, the acquiescence and co-operation upon which peace depends can be shown only through voluntary decisions and joint action. Conflicts of interests and difference in assumptions are likely to be more sharply focused, and there is no higher authority to resolve them. This is the case with contemporary international society. In this situation the immediate alternatives for international organization, aside from the creation of an effective world government by fiat, lie between (1) the principle of self-help expressed through national unilateralism and restricted groupings on the basis of special interests, and (2) the principle of concern expressed through a collective security organization and efforts to implement co-operative action for the maintenance of international peace and security.

The principle of concern was incorporated in international organization with the establishment of the League of Nations. During the next twenty years this principle went through a cycle of acceptance, limitation, modified application, and disintegration. After World War II the principle of concern was reaffirmed, and under the United Nations it has been implemented to a significant extent. This has not been done, however, completely, or even sufficiently, because of the existence of hostile blocs in the place of general co-operation. Joint action based on unanimity of the Great Powers and support of the other members has been replaced by international tensions and the "cold war." But, as F. P. Walters has written,

Before the League, it was held both in theory and practice that every State was the sole and sovereign judge of its own acts, owing no allegiance to any higher authority, entitled to resent criticism or even questioning by other States. Such conceptions have disappeared for ever: it is not doubted, and can never again be doubted, that the community of nations has the moral and legal right to discuss and judge the international conduct of each of its members. The belief that aggressive war is a crime against humanity and that it is the interest, the right and the duty of every State to join in preventing it, is now everywhere taken for granted.[10]

The question for the future is whether a sufficient majority of United Nations members can validate in action the prin-

[10] *A History of the League of Nations*, I, 1-2.

ciples of the Charter, thus laying the foundation for a more effective application of the principle of concern. There is no answer to this question as yet, but one thing is clear: The record of the United Nations in its first eight years was one of response, not withdrawal, in the face of challenge.

Bibliography

In his book on *The League of Nations*, published in 1928, John S. Bassett wrote, "Within the last four years writers interested in the League have given us a number of sound discussions of its various phases with the result that a complete catalogue of their works would assume the form of a considerable monograph" (p. 389). The number of documents, books, and articles concerning the League or the United Nations is now so large that Bassett's statement is in need of amendment by substituting the term "encyclopedia" for "monograph." In view of this fact, the bibliography presented here is limited to an indication of the chief sources which have been used in developing the argument of this book.

1. League of Nations

League of Nations, *Official Journal.*
League of Nations, *Records of the Assembly.*
League of Nations, *Treaty Series.*
League of Nations, *Reports and Resolutions on the Subject of Article 16 of the Covenant.* Doc. A. 14. 1927. V.
League of Nations, *Reduction of Armaments.* Doc. A. 111 (1), IV (1923).
League of Nations, *Arbitration and Security.* Doc. C. 34. M. 74. 1926. V.
League of Nations, *Arbitration, Security, and Reduction of Armaments.* Doc. C. 708. 1924. IX (C.C.O.1.).
League of Nations, *Report of the Chaco Commission.*
League of Nations Secretariat, *Ten Years of World Cooperation.* Geneva, 1930.
Bassett, John S., *The League of Nations: A Chapter in World Politics.* New York: Longmans, Green, 1928.
Burton, Margaret E., *The Assembly of the League of Nations.* Chicago: University of Chicago Press, 1941.
Conwell-Evans, T. P., *The League Council in Action.* London: Oxford University Press, 1929.

Engel, S., "League Reform: An Analysis of Official Proposals and Discussions, 1936-1939," *Geneva Studies*, XI, nos. 3-4 (1940).

Fleming, Denna F., *The United States and the League of Nations, 1918-1920*. New York: Putnam's, 1932.

Howard-Ellis, Charles, *The Origin, Structure & Working of the League of Nations*. Boston: Houghton Mifflin, 1928.

Keris, Georges Le Brun, *Les Projets de Reforme de la Société des Nations et le Developpement du Pacte*. Paris: A. Pedone, 1938.

Kirkpatrick, Helen Paull, "The League and the Chaco Dispute," *Foreign Policy Reports*, XII (1936), 109-20.

Kirkpatrick, Helen Paull, "The Chaco Dispute," *Geneva Studies*, VII, no. 4 (1936), 22-43.

Knudson, John I., *A History of the League of Nations*. Atlanta: T. E. Smith & Co., 1938.

Martelli, George, *Italy Against the World*. London: Chatto & Windus, 1938.

Mattison, Mary, "The Chaco Arms Embargo," *Geneva Studies*, V, no. 5 (1934), 3-16.

Miller, David Hunter, *The Drafting of the Covenant*. 2 vols. New York: Putnam's, 1928.

Morley, Felix, *The Society of Nations*. Washington: Brookings Institution, 1932.

Rappard, William E., *The Geneva Experiment*. London: Oxford University Press, 1931.

Ray, Jean, *Commentaire du Pacte de la Société des Nations*. Paris: Librairie du Recueil Sirey, 1930.

Rhoads, Grace E., "Amendments of the Covenant of the League of Nations Adopted and Proposed." Unpublished dissertation, Bryn Mawr College, 1935.

Schwarzenberger, Georg, "An Analysis of the Replies to Our Questionnaire on the *De Facto* Revision of the Covenant," *New Commonwealth Quarterly*, IV (1938), 60-74.

Schwarzenberger, Georg, "The States Members of the League and the Reform of the Covenant," *New Commonwealth Quarterly*, II (1936), 351-59; III (1937), 271-72.

Walters, F. P., *A History of the League of Nations*. 2 vols. London: Oxford University Press, 1952.

Webster, Charles K., *The League of Nations in Theory and Practice*. London: G. Allen & Unwin, 1933.

Williams, John Fischer, *Some Aspects of the Covenant of the League of Nations*. London: Oxford University Press, 1934.

Williams, John Fischer, "Sovereignty, Seisin and the League," *British Yearbook of International Law*, VII (1936), 24-42.

Willoughby, Westel W., *The Sino-Japanese Controversy and the League of Nations*. Baltimore: Johns Hopkins Press, 1935.
Zahler, Walter H., "Switzerland and the League of Nations," *American Political Science Review*, XXX (1936), 753-57.
Zimmern, Alfred E., *The League of Nations and the Rule of Law*. London: Macmillan, 1936.

2. UNITED NATIONS

United Nations Bulletin (now *United Nations Review*).
United Nations Yearbook.
United Nations, *Annual Reports of the Secretary-General*.
Eagleton, Clyde, and Swift, Richard N. (eds.), *Annual Review of United Nations Affairs*. New York: New York University Press, 1949-1953.
Evatt, Herbert Vere, *The United Nations*. Cambridge, Mass.: Harvard University Press, 1948.
Feller, A. H., *United Nations and World Community*. Boston: Little, Brown, 1952.
Goodrich, Leland M., and Hambro, Edvard, *Charter of the United Nations: Commentary and Documents*. 2nd ed. Boston: World Peace Foundation, 1949.
United States Department of State, *United States Participation in the United Nations* (annual reports of the President to Congress).
Vandenbosch, Amry, and Hogan, Willard N., *The United Nations*. New York: McGraw-Hill, 1952.

3. GENERAL

American Journal of International Law, XVIII (1924), XXIII (1929), XXVI (1932), XXVII (1933), XXX (1936), XXXII (1938).
Berber, F. J. (ed.), *Locarno: A Collection of Documents*. London: Wm. Hodge & Co., 1936.
Bourquin, Maurice (ed.), *Collective Security: A Record of the Seventh and Eighth International Studies Conferences*. Paris: International Institute of Intellectual Co-operation, 1936.
Carr, Edward H., *International Relations between the Two World Wars, 1919-1939*. New York: Macmillan, 1947.
Cohn, Georg, *Neo-Neutrality*. New York: Columbia University Press, 1939.
Cole, Taylor, "Recognition, International," in *Encyclopedia of the Social Sciences*, XIII, 165-68.
Cooper, Russell M., *American Consultation in World Affairs for the*

Preservation of Peace. New York: Macmillan, 1934.

Fifth International Conference of American States, *Verbatim Record of the Plenary Sessions*, II. Santiago, 1923.

Fleming, Denna F., *The United States and World Organization, 1920-1933*. New York: Columbia University Press, 1938.

Friedrich, Carl J., *Foreign Policy in the Making*. New York: W. W. Norton & Co., 1938.

Friedrich, Carl J., *War: The Causes, Effects, and Control of International Violence*. Washington: National Council for the Social Studies, 1943.

Glasgow, George, *From Dawes to Locarno*. New York: Harper, 1926.

Great Britain, Foreign Office, *Statement by the Right Hon. Austen Chamberlain, M.P., on Behalf of His Majesty's Government, to the Council of the League of Nations, respecting the Protocol for the Pacific Settlement of International Disputes*. Cmd. 2368. London, 1925.

Grotius Society, *Transactions*, XVIII (1933).

Hemleben, Sylvester J., *Plans for World Peace through Six Centuries*. Chicago: University of Chicago Press, 1943.

Hill, Chesney, "Recent Policies of Non-Recognition," *International Conciliation*, no. 293 (October, 1933).

Hudson, Manley O., *By Pacific Means*. New Haven: Yale University Press, 1935.

Hudson, Manley O. (ed.), *International Legislation*. 6 vols. Washington: Carnegie Endowment for International Peace, 1931-1937.

International Law Association, *Briand-Kellogg Pact of Paris: Articles of Interpretation as Adopted by the Budapest Conference, 1934*. London: Sweet & Maxwell, 1934.

International Organization (quarterly published by the World Peace Foundation).

Kelsen, Hans, *Peace Through Law*. Chapel Hill: University of North Carolina Press, 1944.

Langer, Robert, *Seizure of Territory*. Princeton: Princeton University Press, 1947.

Loewenstein, Karl, *Political Reconstruction*. New York: Macmillan, 1946.

Manning, C. W. (ed.), *Peaceful Change*. New York: Macmillan, 1937.

Marriott, John A. R., *Commonwealth or Anarchy?* New York: Columbia University Press, 1939.

Miller, David Hunter, *The Geneva Protocol*. New York: Macmillan, 1925.

Miller, David Hunter, *The Peace Pact of Paris*. New York: Putnam's, 1928.

Morgenthau, Hans, *Politics among Nations*. 2nd ed. New York: Knopf, 1954.

Myers, Denys P., *Origin and Conclusion of the Paris Pact*. Boston: World Peace Foundation, 1929.

Neumann, Sigmund, *The Future in Perspective*. New York: Putnam's, 1946.

Nicolson, Harold, *The Congress of Vienna*. London: Constable & Co., 1946.

Noel-Baker, P. J., *Disarmament*. London: Hogarth Press, 1926.

Noel-Baker, P. J., *The Geneva Protocol for the Pacific Settlement of International Disputes*. London: P. S. King & Son, 1925.

Quigley, Harold, *From Versailles to Locarno*. Minneapolis: University of Minnesota Press, 1927.

Rappard, William E., *International Relations as Viewed from Geneva*. New Haven: Yale University Press, 1925.

Rappard, William E., *The Quest for Peace since the World War*. Cambridge, Mass.: Harvard University Press, 1940.

Rappard, William E., *Uniting Europe*. London: Oxford University Press, 1930.

Royal Institute of International Affairs, *Documents on International Affairs, 1935, 1936*. London: Oxford University Press, 1937.

Royal Institute of International Affairs, *International Sanctions*. London: Oxford University Press, 1938.

Salter, Arthur, *Security: Can We Retrieve It?* New York: Macmillan, 1939.

Salvin, Marina, "Soviet Policy Toward Disarmament," *International Conciliation*, no. 428 (February, 1947).

Schuman, Frederick L., *The Commonwealth of Man*. New York: Knopf, 1952.

Schuman, Frederick L., *International Politics*. 5th ed. New York: McGraw-Hill, 1953.

Schwarzenberger, Georg, *Power Politics*. 2nd ed. New York: Praeger, 1951.

Seventh International Conference of American States, *Final Act*. Montevideo, 1933.

Shotwell, James T., *On the Rim of the Abyss*. New York: Macmillan, 1936.

Shotwell, James T., *War as an Instrument of National Policy*. New York: Harcourt, Brace, 1929.

Spaight, J. M., *Pseudo-Security*. New York: Longmans, Green, 1928.

Steed, Wickham, *Vital Peace*. London: Constable & Co., 1936.

Stimson, Henry L., *The Pact of Paris: Three Years of Development* (United States Department of State Publication no. 357). Washington, 1932.

Stoner, John E., *S. O. Levinson and the Pact of Paris*. Chicago: University of Chicago Press, 1943.

Taracouzio, T. A., *The Soviet Union and International Law*. New York: Macmillan, 1935.

Thompson, Kenneth W., "Collective Security Reexamined," *American Political Science Review*, XLVII (1953), 753-72.

Toynbee, Arnold J., *Survey of International Affairs, 1935*, II, *Abyssina and Italy*. London: Oxford University Press, 1936.

United States Congress, *Congressional Record*.

United States Department of State, *Press Releases*.

United States Department of State, *Treaty for the Renunciation of War*. Washington, 1933.

United States Department of State, *Treaty Series*.

Welles, Sumner, *Where Are We Heading?* New York: Harper, 1946.

Wheeler-Bennett, John W., *Disarmament and Security since Locarno, 1925-1931*. New York: Macmillan, 1932.

World Organization (a symposium of the Institute on World Organization). Washington: American Council on Public Affairs, 1942.

Wright, Quincy (ed.), *Neutrality and Collective Security*. Chicago: University of Chicago Press, 1936.

Wright, Quincy, *A Study of War*. 2 vols. Chicago: University of Chicago Press, 1942.

www.ingramcontent.com/pod-product-compliance
Lightning Source LLC
Chambersburg PA
CBHW031508270326
41930CB00006B/310